PERSONAL SECTOR EXPENDITURE AND PORTFOLIO DECISIONS

To my parents

Personal Sector Expenditure and Portfolio Decisions

An integrated model

M.J. BUCKLE

*Department of Management Science
and Statistics
University College of Swansea*

Avebury

Aldershot · Brookfield USA · Hong Kong · Singapore · Sydney

Published by
Avebury
Academic Publishing Group
Gower House
Croft Road
Aldershot
Hants. GU11 3HR
England

Gower Publishing Company
Old Post Road
Brookfield
Vermont 05036
USA

A CIP catalogue record for this book is available from the British Library and the US Library of Congress.

ISBN 1 85628 249 X

Printed and Bound in Great Britain by
Athenaeum Press Ltd., Newcastle upon Tyne.

Contents

1 Introduction

This book describes a study with the objective of constructing and estimating a quarterly model of UK
Personal sector expenditure and portfolio decisions for
the period 1976 to 1987. The model that is developed in
this study differs from most other empirical studies of
Personal sector behaviour in that an integrated
framework is adopted for estimation which allows for
simultaneous interrelationships between expenditure and
portfolio decisions. The resulting model will enable a
wide variety of relationships between real and financial
decisions of the Personal sector to be examined.

Previous studies of Personal sector behaviour have in
the main treated consumption decisions as separable
from portfolio decisions and the different parts of portfolio decisions as separable from each other. There are a
number of related reasons which can be advanced to
explain the dominance of this separable approach to
modelling. The lack of a unified theory of portfolio behaviour has been used to justify modelling one part of the
portfolio decision, for example the demand for money,
separately from other parts such as the demand for

government bonds. With regard to the separation of consumption and portfolio modelling, the most popular approach to modelling UK consumption expenditures in recent years has been the "error-correction approach" represented by Hendry (1983). The aim of this approach is to find an accurate dynamic description of aggregate consumption, and whilst an increasing role has been found for wealth variables in this approach it still falls short of the systematic integrated approach adopted in this study. However, probably the main reason why the assumption of separability has been so widely adopted in empirical studies of Personal sector behaviour is that it considerably simplifies the modelling process by allowing the problem to be split into smaller independent parts. The alternative systems approach to modelling demand equations is well known for being fraught with problems, in particular the large number of free parameters to estimate causing a greater potential for multicollinearity resulting in large numbers of poorly defined or implausibly signed coefficients. This makes the resulting model less useful as a framework for policy simulations. There have been a few attempts to model Personal sector decisions using an integrated framework. However these studies also suffered from the above mentioned problems associated with the systems approach to modelling.

It is argued in this study that the assumption of separability invoked in modelling Personal sector decisions results in implausible restrictions on behaviour. Therefore a systems framework that allows fully for inter-relationships between expenditure and financial decisions is adopted in the estimation of the model. The problems associated with systems modelling, mentioned above, are mitigated in this study in two ways. Firstly the restrictions of homogeneity and symmetry of interest rate responses, which are predictions of utility theory, are tested for. These restrictions if accepted by the data reduce the number of coefficients to be estimated and hence the potential for multicollinearity. Secondly the Granger - Engle two step technique is adopted for estimating the model. This has a number of advantages over the conventional approach to estimation, in particular that the long run parameters are estimated separately from the dynamic parameters and then held fixed whilst the search for a parsimonious dynamic model takes place. This partial separation of the estimation process further helps to reduce the multicollinearity problem and also allows the restrictions of homogeneity and symmetry to be applied to both the dynamic and long run interest rate parameters.

The plan of this book is as follows. In chapter two the theoretical background to household consumption and portfolio behaviour is discussed. In particular the assumption of separability is critically examined. In chapter three previous attempts to model household expenditure and portfolio behaviour are surveyed. This survey as one would anticipate from this introduction is essentially split into two parts, namely a survey of consumption modelling and a survey of portfolio modelling. The few previous attempts at integrated modelling are also considered with the main emphasis here being on the difficulties associated with applying the integrated approach. In chapter four the problems of constructing a data set for estimating the proposed model are examined. A related question of the scope of the model, in terms of which portfolio decisions are to be included, is also addressed. Chapter five contains a discussion of trends in the data used for estimation. In chapter six the specification of the model is described and two approaches to estimation are compared. For the reasons outlined earlier, the Granger - Engle two step approach is adopted and the results of the estimation are presented and discussed. Simulation experiments using the model are reported in chapter seven. A major policy issue examined is the effects of direct controls on credit compared to altering rates of interest. In chapter eight the study as a whole is reviewed.

2 Theoretical background

2.1 Introduction

In this chapter the main elements of economic theory concerned with the consumption and portfolio behaviour of households or individuals will be surveyed. In the first section the original formulation of the Life Cycle Hypothesis is outlined and recent modifications to this formulation arising from the relaxation of the assumption of perfect capital markets are discussed. In the next section the various theories advanced to explain the portfolio decisions of households are discussed. The view is advanced that there exists a number of different approaches to modelling the various parts of household portfolio decision making and that so far no unified theory has emerged. It is argued that this lack of a unified theory is one reason to explain why most empirical work on modelling household portfolio decisions invokes the assumption of separability of preferences. In the final section this assumption of separability is examined and the question as to whether it is legitimate to view the different parts of the portfolio decision as

4

separate from each other and from the consumption decision is considered.

2.2 Theories of consumption

Two principal theories concerned with explaining consumption behaviour are the Permanent Income Hypothesis and the Life Cycle Hypothesis. Both theories are based upon intertemporal utility maximising behaviour on the part of households. Both theories assume that households current consumption is related to its total resources (equal to the present value of all future income expected from human and non-human sources). The difference between the two theories is one of emphasis in that the Life Cycle Hypothesis is concerned explicitly with the role of asset accumulation and the effect of age on household consumption. The similarity of these two theories allows for the consideration of only one of these theories as representative of consumption theory and the explicit role for asset accumulation leads to a choice of the Life Cycle Hypothesis which is now discussed.

The Life Cycle Hypothesis (LCH) of consumption (Modigliani and Brumberg, (1955)), proposes that households, in general, plan their lifetime consumption patterns so as to maximise total utility derived over their lifetime. In the simple version of the LCH, households will save and hence accumulate assets during times of highest income (usually middle age) and dis-save when income is lowest. Thus the motive for saving in the LCH is to flatten the lifetime profile of consumption expenditures and avoid restrictions imposed by a varying level of income. In the LCH, aggregate consumption is principally a function of expected lifetime wealth (both human and non-human) and given the assumption of perfect capital markets, a household can freely borrow against both types of wealth. An implication of perfect capital markets is that the composition of a households assets does not influence its consumption behaviour. So redistribution of a households assets that leaves the total

5

value of its wealth unaltered will not influence its consumption. Since the original formulation of the LCH a significant literature has appeared dealing with implications when the assumption of perfect capital markets is relaxed. The three forms of capital market imperfection considered here are (i) constraints on borrowing, (ii) transaction costs and (iii) uncertainty. Turning to the first imperfection, in practice households will find it difficult to borrow against assets that are mainly held in illiquid form - human wealth as well as non-human wealth such as retirement benefits. When a household faces constraints on borrowing then consumption defined by their optimal lifetime consumption plan will not be achievable. Such households will find their consumption expenditure more closely related to receipts of income and those parts of wealth that are most liquid, and are termed liquidity constrained households. Tobin (1972) argues that liquidity constrained households will behave differently when compared to non-constrained households. In particular, they will tend to have higher net assets, a higher marginal propensity to consume and will not alter current consumption patterns in response to marginal changes in illiquid resources and small changes in interest rates. Tobin and Dolde (1974) found liquidity constraints to be binding on poorer sections of the community and many of those in younger age groups. In analysing aggregate consumption behaviour it is therefore likely that there exists a significant number of households which face borrowing constraints, although there will be differing degrees of constraint. Whilst it is difficult to assess the number of households facing borrowing constraints it is likely that the number facing borrowing constraints will be related to the extent of controls on borrowing and the availability of credit. Thus the number of borrowing constrained households will vary over the period of study (1976 to 1987) and is likely to have reduced since the early 1980's (ignoring demographic and other factors) as credit controls have diminished. One implication of liquidity constrained behaviour is that in modelling aggregate consumption, current income as well as wealth is likely to be an important determinant. Also the composition and not just the level of wealth will be important, with the liquid asset component an important determinant for liquidity constrained households. This conclusion is arrived at by a different route by Pissarides (1978), who examined the implications of transactions costs for the LCH and it is this to which we now turn.

Given the assumption of perfect capital markets in the LCH, then the maximisation of a utility function defined over commodities and assets implies that the composition of commodity and asset endowments does not influence consumption i.e. redistribution of an individuals asset portfolio, given no change in the size of the portfolio does not influence consumption. With the introduction of transaction costs in capital markets, and given that consumers are aware of these costs, then, argues Pissarides (1978), it will be cheaper to finance consumption by running down liquid assets than, for example, by selling long term assets before maturity or while there are surrender costs. It follows therefore that the composition of the portfolio will be chosen simultaneously with the optimal consumption plan in such a way as to enable the realisation of all desired consumption at the lowest possible transaction costs.

With respect to the third imperfection, uncertainty, in the LCH households are assumed to know with certainty their future lifetime income stream thus enabling the process of inter-temporal utility maximisation. One implication of relaxing this assumption has already been considered i.e. when future income is uncertain then borrowing against it becomes more difficult. Attempts have been made to extend the LCH to allow for uncertainty (see Merton (1969) and Dreze and Modigliani (1972)). An alternative hypothesis about consumption and asset accumulation which makes uncertainty a central feature is the wealth hypothesis presented and developed by Spiro (1962), Ball and Drake (1964) and Clower and Johnson (1968). Once uncertainty enters the analysis the household then safeguards against this by accumulating assets. Thus saving and hence asset accumulation, in this hypothesis, is not related to some notion of lifetime consumption but more to a broad precautionary motive.

Therefore a relationship between consumption expenditures and asset accumulation can be established on theoretical grounds when the assumptions of perfect capital markets and certainty about the future are relaxed and transactions costs are introduced into the analysis. We now turn to consider the main theories concerned with the portfolio decision.

2.3 Theories of the portfolio decision

The theories in this area fall into one of three broad categories. These are transaction or inventory theoretic, precautionary and mean-variance models. These three categories of theories are generally applied to demand for money modelling, but as will be seen in chapter three, the last two have been applied to the modelling of a wider set of asset demands. It is argued that the characteristic of money as a means of exchange leads to transaction models and its role as a store of value leads to portfolio models.

Transaction models, first presented by Baumol (1952) and Tobin (1956), are based on the notion that an economic agent tries to organise its money balances so as to minimise the cost of its known transactions. This approach assumes that agents continuously adjust money balances in order to remain at their optimal level. This seems unlikely for individuals. Akerlof and Milbourne (1980) develop a model in the broad tradition of transaction models based on the more realistic assumption that individuals only actively adjust their money balances when they reach an upper or lower target level. Transaction models attempt to explain the motives for holding only one asset, namely money (however defined), and they generally assume certainty of income and expenditures. In contrast precautionary models (mentioned earlier - in the broader sense of motives for holding wealth - in the wealth hypothesis) assume uncertainty of future net receipts. In such models, an agent faces a cost if payments net of receipts are greater than money holdings. The cost arises from "distress" sales of assets i.e. selling assets at short notice which involves time, possible interest loss, surrender costs etc. On the other hand, holding a higher level of money balances than required incurs a loss of return on higher yielding assets or a reduction in consumption opportunities. Miller and Orr (1966 and 1968) introduce the notion of a band of money holdings and it is only when the upper or lower limit of this band is reached that adjustments are made. Optimal buffer stock theory is also concerned with behaviour aimed at maintaining the lower band to cash holdings. In a further development of this approach Markose (1984), in the context of a precautionary model, argues that the stochastic nature of investment opportunities and the state dependence of asset prices (i.e. asset prices and rates of return depend on stochastic exogenous state variables such as inflation, real income etc.) implies that individuals will hold assets as a hedge against unfavourable shifts in the exogenous state variables.

The third approach to portfolio behaviour is the mean-variance approach which is based on the notion that individuals like wealth but are averse to risk. Thus in choosing the amount of each asset they wish to hold in a portfolio, individuals will trade off risk (uncertain future value - measured in terms of the standard deviation of the distribution of returns) against expected return. In this approach, the notion of a diversified portfolio is thus introduced and Tobin (1958) has developed a model whereby money is held in the portfolio in order to reduce the overall riskiness of the portfolio. There has been some debate in the literature though as to whether the mean-variance approach can be used to explain non interest bearing holdings of money. It is argued that where short term interest bearing assets of low risk exist then it is difficult to explain holdings of non interest bearing money within a portfolio using the mean-variance approach (see Sprenkle (1984), and Chang et al (1984)).

The mean variance approach is criticised (see Deaton and Muellbauer, 1980a), firstly because it is based on the assumption of normally distributed yields - which rarely occur in practice - and secondly, because it relies on the assumption of a quadratic utility function which implies that the rich insure more heavily than the poor against the same risk and that the rich hold more cash and less risky assets (absolutely) than do the poor. Also the informational requirements in using the mean-variance approach to explain asset holdings may limit its use to sophisticated financial firms such as banks and investment institutions. Finally the holdings of risky (uncertain capital value) assets by the Personal Sector are small relative to total assets and these holdings are not widely held within the Personal Sector.

Thus it would appear that a variety of approaches exist to explain the portfolio decision of households, with little common ground between them. There have been a few attempts to combine these different approaches to modelling the portfolio decision. One example is the work of Buiter and Armstrong (1978) who develop a Baumol type transactions model within a mean-variance framework. However the more usual approach to the problem of modelling the different motives for the holding of assets has been to invoke the assumption of preference separability. The implications of invoking this assumption will be considered later. First, the nature of the separability assumption will be outlined.

2.4 Separability of preferences

The notion of separability of preferences was developed in the context of constructing commodity groupings in relation to modelling consumption of different commodities. (see Strotz (1957), (1959), Gorman (1959) and Deaton & Muellbauer (1980a)). If separability of preferences holds then commodities can be partitioned into groups so that preferences within groups can be described independently of the quantities in other groups. Thus we obtain sub-utility functions for the separate groups and the values of each of these sub-utilities combine to give total utility. Each group may also have one or more deeper sub-groupings within it. This can be shown in terms of a utility tree - shown below :

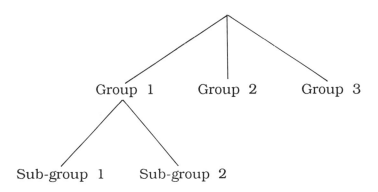

Figure 2.1 : A utility tree

A related idea, suggested by the diagram, is that of two stage budgeting. That is, a consumer can allocate total expenditure over commodities in two stages. In stage 1 expenditure is allocated to groups 1 to 3. In the second stage group expenditure is then allocated to the sub-groups. At each stage information appropriate to that stage only, is required for the allocation decision. Thus it becomes possible to model the demand for one sub-group without reference to the determinants of the other sub-groups. The separability just described is generally termed weak separability and invoking its assumption places severe restrictions on the degree of substitutability between commodities in different groups (see page 13).

We now consider the separability assumption and the utility tree in relation to the consumption - portfolio decision :

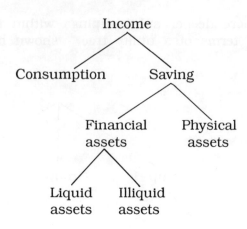

Figure 2.2: A utility tree for household consumption -
portfolio decisions

Demand for an asset within the sub-group liquid assets will depend on returns on liquid assets and on the allocation of savings to liquid assets and is independent of the returns on illiquid assets. Thus the separability assumption allows single equation estimation of demand for sub-sets of total wealth with a smaller number of explanatory variables. Therefore in relation to the modelling of portfolio decisions of individuals it is possible to assume that individuals decisions about their demand for equities can be made independently of their decisions concerning demand for building society deposits.

At the first stage of the allocation in the utility tree shown above, allocation between consumption and saving is determined by, among other things income. This raises the question as to whether income is exogenous or endogenous. For some individuals it is possible to alter the number of hours worked and so for these individuals income should be a treated as a choice variable. In considering aggregate behaviour this may be less important and in empirical studies it is rare to see income treated as a choice variable because of the econometric implications. The other determinants of this first stage are appropriately defined group prices for consumption and savings. Hence interest rates on assets (or a composite of interest rates) should appear as a determinant of the consumption/saving allocation decision. In empirical studies of the consumption function interest rate variables are often excluded. This is because most empirical studies of the consumption function treat saving as a residual. However once it is recognised that saving is a purposeful act then the behavioural determinants of saving should enter the consumption function. Some of the motives for saving have already been mentioned, for example, to spread consumption, to hedge against future uncertainty. These motives can be pursued in a variety of forms, that is by holding different types of assets. The determinants of the holding of these different types of assets should therefore influence the consumption - savings decision.

The assumption of separability of preferences is a commonly adopted assumption in empirical studies (although it is not always made explicit). It permits the modelling of portfolio decisions with the consumption/saving decision pre-determined. It permits the modelling of a sub-group of assets without the need to allow for possible linkages with other sub-groups of assets. Thus the advantage of invoking the separability assumption is that it simplifies the modelling process.

It is argued here that separable preferences and two stage budgeting impose implausible restrictions on behaviour, in particular the restrictions imposed on substitution between groups. There will clearly be substitution between expenditure on items in the consumption group and the allocation of funds to the financial or physical asset sub-group. For example a household that purchases a car may cut down consumption expenditure on bus and train fares. There may also be substitution between sub-groups of financial assets. For example if financial assets are separated into liquid and illiquid assets then this restricts possible substitution between say building society deposits and ordinary shares.

Thus a view of household decision making where real and financial decisions are integrated and where interrelationships between decisions are allowed for will be the central theme of this research. This can be achieved by defining simultaneously interdependent consumption and asset demand behavioural relationships.

2.5 Conclusion

Saving and hence wealth accumulation is postulated to arise from the desire of individuals or households to smooth consumption spending over their lifetime. In addition, a precautionary motive, arising from the existence of unforeseen fluctuations of income etc. would lead to the holding of a non-zero stock of non-human wealth.

It was shown in the discussion of theories of consumption behaviour that consumption and asset accumulation by households are interrelated and more importantly that the composition of the household's portfolio will be determined jointly with consumption plans. In the discussion of theories of the portfolio decision the view was put forward that the theories developed attempt to explain only parts of the total portfolio of households and that no theory is applicable to all parts of the portfolio decision. This has led to the invoking of the separability of preferences assumption in empirical work on portfolio behaviour. The separability assumption also allows the modelling of consumption separately from portfolio behaviour. However, it was argued that the restrictions implied by the separable consumption - portfolio decision making are not justifiable. Thus the central feature of this research will be the modelling of households consumption and portfolio behaviour in an integrated framework that allows for simultaneous interrelationships.

In the next chapter, previous attempts at modelling households consumption and portfolio behaviour will be surveyed and the implications for modelling this behaviour in a simultaneous framework will be investigated.

3 Modelling households consumption and portfolio decisions

3.1 Introduction

In the previous chapter it was noted that most attempts to model households consumption and portfolio decisions invoke the separability of preferences assumption in order to reduce the inter-relationships between decisions and so simplify the modelling process. It was also stated that the approach taken in this research is not to assume separability but to investigate the problems and advantages of modelling households consumption and portfolio behaviour in an integrated framework that allows for simultaneous inter-relationships between real and financial decisions. The objective of this chapter is to survey the empirical literature on the modelling of households consumption and portfolio decisions. In the first section the main approach adopted in recent modelling of UK consumption behaviour will be discussed. It is argued here that despite an increasing emphasis on wealth effects in modelling consumption behaviour there is still a dichotomy in the literature when it comes to modelling consumption and portfolio behaviour. In the second section which considers the modelling of portfolio decisions, the view presented is that in much of this work, not only are portfolio decisions seen as separate from consumption decisions but that the different parts of the portfolio decision are modelled separately. There is a voluminous empirical literature concerned with portfolio modelling and clearly it is not practicable to summarise it all and therefore the survey in this section concentrates on the modelling of systems of asset demands as this has more relevance to the approach adopted in this study. In the third section the few attempts that have been made to jointly model consumption and portfolio demands are considered together with an examination of some of the practical problems of applying the integrated approach. In the final section the lessons for this study arising out of this discussion of previous empirical work are reviewed.

3.2 Modelling consumption

In the main, recent empirical modelling of the aggregate consumption function in the UK has adopted one of two competing approaches. These may be classified as rational expectations models and "error-correction models". The rational expectations models are based on the stochastic life cycle or permanent income hypothesis and a key assumption is that agents form rational expectations about the key decision variables (see for example Hall (1978)). The "error-correction models" use econometric techniques in order to specify a relationship which captures the dynamics of consumption whilst being consistent with stylized facts about long run behaviour. Both these approaches invoke the separability assumption, however recent studies using the "error-correction approach" have attempted to allow for financial influences on consumption behaviour. The "error-correction approach" is therefore moving closer to the integrated approach adopted in this research and what follows is a brief summary of the "error-correction approach" (for a more detailed summary see Hendry (1983)).

An influential study using the "error-correction approach" was that of Davidson et al (1978), represented in equation [3.1] below, where C, Y and p denote real non-durable consumption, real personal disposable income and the consumer price index respectively.

$$\Delta_4 \log C_t = a_1 \Delta_4 \log Y_t + a_2 \Delta_1 \Delta_4 \log Y_t + a_3 \Delta_4 \log p_t$$
$$+ a_4 \Delta_1 \Delta_4 \log p_t + a_5 \log (C/Y)_{t-4} \qquad [3.1]$$

Hendry and Ungern-Sternberg [HUS],(1981), identify two shortcomings of this model: no allowance for wealth effects and the use of an income measure which is overstated in times of high inflation. In order to develop a model which overcomes these problems [HUS] make the assumption that the Personal Sector form long run desired ratios of consumption to income and wealth to income :

$$(C/Y)_t^* = K$$
$$(W/Y)_t^* = B$$

By minimising a cost function the following equation is derived:

$$\Delta_4 \log C_t = a_1 \Delta_4 \log Y_t + a_2 \Delta_1 \Delta_4 \log Y_t$$
$$+ a_3 \log (C/Y)_{t-4} + a_4 \log(W/Y)_{t-4} \qquad [3.2]$$

Here changes in the consumption of non-durables (C) are modelled as a function of changes in income (Y), acceleration of income, the ratio of consumption to income and a wealth (W) to income ratio. The last term introduces wealth effects and represents an integral control mechanism. The term integral is used because the change in consumption is assumed to depend on the sum (or in continuous time, the integral) of past deviations from equilibrium in the consumption to income ratio. However disequilibrium in the consumption to income ratio in the past may result in disequilibrium in the stock of wealth. It should be noted that this was not the first empirical model of aggregate consumption behaviour to allow for wealth effects. A notable example of a study that also tested wealth variables and so introduced implicitly an integral control mechanism was that of Stone (1973). The overstatement of income problem is overcome in the [HUS] study by adjusting measured income for the erosion of liquid assets caused by inflation (see section 4.4 for further discussion of this). The [HUS] study found no role for a price variable (cf. Davidson et al) as [HUS] argued that inflation effects are captured by inflation adjustment of the income term. A model of the aggregate consumption behaviour of the UK Personal Sector in the tradition of [HUS] is that of Davis (1984)[1]. It is useful to examine this model, not only because it is representative of the "error-correction approach" to modelling the consumption function but also because it is part of a larger model of Personal Sector behaviour in which the separability assumption is invoked. It therefore represents an alternative approach to the one adopted in this study. The specification of the consumption function estimated in the Davis study is essentially that shown in [3.2][2]. Davis, like [HUS] uses net liquid assets as a proxy for wealth in the integral control variable for a number of reasons, including that liquid assets represents a significant proportion of total wealth, it is the part of wealth that is distributed more evenly across households, a long run of data on liquid assets is available and it represents an important source of funds for liquidity constrained households (see chapter 2 for discussion of liquidity constraints). Davis also tested for other wealth variables, including illiquid financial assets, but these were ruled out on statistical grounds. An interest rate term (ie. a determinant of portfolio behaviour) was also tested for but found to be insignificant.

There are a number of issues highlighted by this model. Firstly the separability assumption is invoked in order to simplify the modelling process, however some attempt is made to allow for portfolio influences on consumption behaviour through the lagged net liquid assets term - see figure 3.1

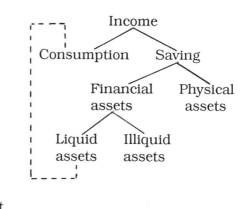

Figure 3.1 : Recursive structure of Davis (1984) model

This recursive structure, though, rules out simultaneous inter-relationships. Secondly only one part of wealth
is allowed to influence consumption behaviour. Other
studies in the [HUS] tradition have found a role for
illiquid financial wealth in the consumption function. For
example Patterson (1984) using a separate illiquid financial asset integral control mechanism and Pesaran and
Evans (1984) using capital gains/losses on illiquid financial assets both found these variables to have a significant effect on consumption. Third, as in most empirical
studies of consumption behaviour no role is found for
interest rates[3]. However, it was argued in chapter 2 that
even when separability of preferences is assumed in
modelling consumption (and by implication savings)
behaviour then determinants of savings behaviour are
still needed in the consumption function. Finally, net
liquid assets (ie. gross liquid assets less bank borrowing
excluding loans for house purchase) is used to represent
the integral control mechanism and this implies that
gross liquid assets and bank borrowing have the same
(lagged) influence on consumption. Davis (1984) does test
a variant of the main model that allows for differential
influences of these two components of net liquid assets,
however the use of net asset variables highlights the
issue of the appropriate level of aggregation of asset

groupings. The aggregation of different types of short term assets into a liquid assets grouping does not allow for differential influences of the components making up the grouping. There may be justifiable reasons for aggregation, but a better approach would be to test for this empirically (see chapter 4 for a discussion of aggregation).

3.3 Modelling portfolio behaviour

Empirical studies of the portfolio decision of households can be seen as falling into two categories; studies of part of the portfolio decision, mainly the demand for money, and studies involving systems of asset demands which attempt to model most or all of the portfolio decisions of households. As discussed in chapter 2, there exists no complete theory of households portfolio decisions so the latter systems approach empirical studies, with some exceptions, have tended to be based on 'eclectic' models. It is the attempts to model most or all of households portfolio decisions that will now be considered, beginning with those studies which can be regarded as exceptions to the more usual 'eclectic' approach.

Barrett, Gray and Parkin (1975) developed a model of the demand for financial assets by the Personal Sector of the UK, based on the precautionary approach. The separability assumption is invoked allowing the modelling of 'safe' financial assets independently from the (not modelled) demand for 'risky' assets. The structuring of decisions underlying this approach is shown in figure 3.2 below :

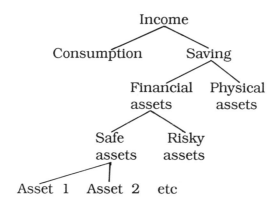

Figure 3.2 : Structure of Barrett, Gray and Parkin
(1975) model

Thus only part (albeit a large part) of the portfolio decisions of households are modelled.

There have been a number of attempts to apply the mean-variance approach to portfolio modelling, although most of these have been applications to financial institutions, for example, Parkin (1970) and Courakis (1975) apply a static mean-variance model to UK discount houses, Parkin, Gray and Barrett (1970) apply a static mean-variance model to UK commercial banks, White (1975), Berndt, McCurdy and Rose (1980) and Bewley (1981) extend the Parkin et al study. Spencer (1981) has applied the mean variance approach to the modelling of the demand for British Government Stocks by non-bank residents. It was mentioned in chapter 2 that the information requirements assumed by the mean-variance approach limits its applicability to sophisticated agents and this no doubt accounts for the application to the portfolio decisions of financial institutions rather than the personal sector, which is the subject of this study.

Turning now to what may be termed the 'eclectic' approach to modelling the portfolio decisions of households. Brainard and Tobin (1968) developed a model of asset accumulation for all sectors of the economy, which has since been widely applied and extended. In this model it is hypothesised that economic agents have some desired relationship between their holdings of individual financial assets[4] and some measure of their wealth, this relationship being some function of the interest rates on the components of their asset and liability portfolio. This can be expressed as:

$$A_j^* = \sum_{k=0}^{m} \beta_{jk} \cdot X_k \qquad j=1 \text{ to } n \qquad [3.3]$$

where A_j^* = desired demand for asset j, X_m is wealth at the end of the period, X_0 is income and X_k (k=1 to m-1) are rates of return on assets and any other variables that may influence the determination of desired asset stocks. Brainard and Tobin consider a form of [3.3]

$$A_j^* = (\sum_{k=0}^{m-1} \beta_{jk} \cdot X_k) \cdot X_m \qquad [3.4]$$

The role of the wealth homogeneity constraint is to require that any shift in an asset's share of the desired portfolio is due to movements in interest rates rather than to overall growth in the portfolio itself. Its adoption allows the possibility of assuming that the personal sector seek to maintain desired shares of assets in total wealth (i.e. A_j^*/X_m), or if income homogeneity is assumed then desired asset shares in income (ie. A_j^*/X_0). In the latter case this represents an extension of the assumption of a desired wealth to income ratio made in the [HUS] study - see section 3.2 earlier. While such assumptions may be theoretically desirable it needs to be borne in mind that the assumption of homogeneity of wealth is a strong assumption. As de Leeuw (1965) argues homogeneity with respect to money values of wealth implies, in general, homogeneity with respect to both real values of wealth and the price level. While the latter is quite plausible (though ruling out money illusion) the former is much less plausible as it does not allow for the not unlikely situation of disproportionate changes in desired holdings of an asset to changes in real wealth when income and other explanatory variables are held constant. However this assumption can easily be tested for and is therefore an empirical matter.

It is also generally hypothesised in the eclectic approach that where the actual stock of any asset does not equal the desired stock, adjustment to the desired level does not take place instantaneously, but gradually, with the change in any period depending in part on the discrepancy between desired and actual stocks. This adjustment behaviour follows given the existence of adjustment costs discussed below. Brainard and Tobin extended this adjustment mechanism to cover the multi-asset case. Here they proposed an adjustment mechanism which makes changes in the ith asset depend not only on the 'own' asset discrepancy between actual and desired stocks, but also on the discrepancy between actual and desired stocks in all other assets in the portfolio. Thus an inter-dependent asset adjustment mechanism is proposed (ie. separability of asset demands is not assumed). Failure to specify these dynamic cross adjustment effects, argue Brainard and Tobin, may result in unintended consequences for the omitted (residual) equation[5].

The multi-asset partial adjustment framework can be specified as :

$$\Delta A_{it} = A_{it} - A_{it-1} = \sum_{j=1}^{n} \gamma_{ij} (A_{jt}^{*} - A_{jt-1}) + \partial \Delta W \qquad [3.5]$$

As Smith (1975) has pointed out, equation [3.5] over-describes the portfolio adjustment process and thus the term $\partial \Delta W$, representing new wealth, is redundant and can be dropped[6].

Substituting [3.3] into [3.5] yields the following n reduced form asset demand equations for estimation:

$$\Delta A_{i} = \sum_{k=0}^{m} \alpha_{ik} X_{k} - \sum_{j=1}^{n} \gamma_{ij} A_{jt-1} \qquad [3.6]$$

where the impact multipliers given by $\alpha_{ik} = \Sigma_j \gamma_{ij} \cdot \Sigma_j \beta_{jk}$ denote the total impact effect of a change in the kth explanatory variable on the flow demand for the ith asset.

The following set of conditions apply to this model:

$$\sum_{i=1}^{n} \alpha_{ik} = 0 \qquad \text{for } i=0 \text{ to } m-1 \qquad (a)$$

$$\sum_{i=1}^{n} \alpha_{im} = 1 \qquad\qquad (b)$$

$$\sum_{i=1}^{n} \gamma_{ij} = 1 \qquad \text{for } j=1 \text{ to } n \qquad (c)$$

These conditions reflect firstly that demands must satisfy the wealth constraint (often called the adding up constraint), and secondly the treatment of wealth as exogenous. Thus (a) shows that changes in interest rates lead only to a reshuffling of assets since wealth is explicitly held constant. Condition (b) shows that an increase in wealth must induce an equivalent increase in asset holdings. Condition (c) implies that any reshuffling of initial assets, holding initial wealth constant, does not necessarily influence current wealth.

Christophodes (1976) has shown that equations such as [3.5] may be derived from minimising the (quadratic) costs of being out of equilibrium and of adjustment costs, for all assets, that is by minimising:

$$C = \Sigma \, \epsilon_i \, (A_i - A_i^*)^2 + \Sigma \, \eta_i \, (A_i - A_{it-1})^2 \qquad [3.7]$$

subject to the rational desires hypothesis $\Sigma \, A_i^* = W$

A more general version of the cost function has been adopted in some studies of asset demands (for example

Hood, (1987)) to model the costs of being out of equilibrium :

$$C = \Sigma \, \epsilon_i \, (A_i - A_i^*)^2 + \Sigma \, \eta_i \, (A_i - A_{it-1})^2$$
$$- \Sigma \, \omega_i \, (A_i - A_i^*)(A_i - A_{it-1}) \qquad [3.8]$$

The third term in the cost function described by [3.8], a negatively signed interaction term, is included on the grounds that costs will be less if desired and actual levels of A_t are moving in the same direction. An implication of quadratic costs of adjustment is that costs rise smoothly with the size of transaction undertaken. This is clearly unrealistic with regard to financial assets. However er an alternative interpretation is that the quadratic cost function simply characterises sluggish adjustment.

The estimation of such a set of equations as [3.6] is relatively straightforward. Either OLS or instrumental variables applied to each equation separately will automatically satisfy the adding up constraints if all equations contain the same independent variables (this also leads to the OLS estimates being equivalent to estimates obtained using seemingly unrelated regression estimation, SURE). It is also possible to adjust for autocorrelation on an equation by equation basis, provided that equal autocorrelation coefficients are acceptable for each equation. It has to be noted though that if particular variables are excluded from one or a sub-set of equations (say, if estimated coefficients are insignificant) then restricted estimation is necessary to impose the adding up constraint. Also the equations of a system such as [3.6] must be linear in variables in order to satisfy the adding up constraint (the use of log linear variables is possible if approximation of the adding up constraint is acceptable). A limited number of attempts to estimate such a model have been made and these include Backus, Brainard, Smith and Tobin (1980) for the complete (ie. all sectors modelled simultaneously) US economy and Green (1982) similarly for the UK. The problems of applying the multivariate stock adjustment model are considered later in this chapter.

The literature surveyed so far has only considered the

implications of transaction costs on dynamic adjustment of asset stocks to the equilibrium position. There are other implications of transaction costs on the portfolio decision. Such costs include both the direct and pecuniary charges such as brokerage fees and the more indirect costs of time involved in trading and of gathering and processing information. One implication of these transaction costs is that it is less costly to allocate new cash flows - including new savings, payments such as interest and dividends and assets just matured - than to re-allocate existing wealth holdings. It therefore follows that the simple adjustment framework represented by equation [3.5] is inadequate in failing to distinguish between allocation of new cash flows and re-allocation of existing wealth. Friedman (1977) addresses the problem by developing a model which incorporates this distinction in a tractable way: the optimal marginal adjustment model, represented by:

$$\Delta A_{it} = \sum_j \theta_{ij} \left(\alpha_{jt}^* \, W_{t-1} - A_{jt-1} \right) + \alpha_{it}^* \, \Delta W_t \qquad [3.9]$$

$$\text{where } \theta_{ij} = \theta \quad \text{for all } j$$

$$\text{and } \alpha_{it}^* = A_{it}^* \, / \, W$$

The first term on the right hand side represents re-allocation of existing wealth, W_{t-1}, in terms of the discrepancy between desired and actual wealth (both own and cross discrepancies as in [3.5]). The second represents the flow allocation of new wealth in accordance with the desired portfolio share for that asset. This assumes that there are no costs involved with the allocation of new wealth which can therefore be allocated fully in accordance with the desired portfolio share (derived from [3.3]). The inclusion of the term $\alpha_{it}^* \Delta W_t$ in equation [3.9] makes it possible to sign, a priori, some of the long run coefficients and identify them from estimation of a single asset demand equation. This is not possible with the Brainard-Tobin approach where n-1 of the n equations in the system have to be estimated to identify long run parameters. This feature of the optimal marginal adjustment model makes it very suitable for modelling supply and demand functions across a market without the need to model each sectors complete set of portfolio decisions. Hence variations of the optimal marginal adjustment model have been applied to the US corporate bond market (Friedman, (1977), Friedman and Roley, (1979) - the latter study extends the earlier by examining the role of expectations for bond demands). However there are practical drawbacks to adopting the optimal marginal adjustment model to modelling complete portfolio demands for a sector such as with this study. These problems are briefly considered later in this chapter.

3.4 Joint modelling of consumption and portfolio behaviour

The Brainard-Tobin and optimal marginal adjustment models are attempting to model the portfolio decision only - that is, the allocation of savings (new wealth) and the re-allocation of existing wealth. The allocation of income to consumption/savings is taken as given. However the central theme of this research, developed in chapter 2, is that economic agents choose the composition of their portfolio simultaneously with their optimal consumption plan. Therefore an appropriate model is one that allows for simultaneous interrelationships between the consumption - savings decision and the portfolio decision.

One such model has been developed by Purvis (1978), and extended by Smith (1978) and Owen (1981). The Purvis model extends the Brainard-Tobin model (represented by equations [3.3], [3.5] and [3.6] described earlier), to allow for integrated expenditure and portfolio behaviour.

This model is represented as:

$$A_j^* = \sum_{k=0}^{m-1} \beta_{jk} X_k \qquad [3.10]$$

$$\Delta A_i = \sum_{j=1}^{n} \gamma_{ij} (A_{jt}^* - A_{jt-1}) \qquad [3.11]$$

$$C = \sum_{k=0}^{m-1} b_k X_k + \sum_{j=1}^{n} e_j A_{jt-1} \qquad [3.12]$$

where A_j^* = desired asset demand
C = consumption
X_k = variables explaining A_j^*
(including current income (X_o) and rates of return on assets in the portfolio)

The budget constraint implicit in this model is given by:

$$\sum_{i=1}^{n} A_i + C = \sum_{i=1}^{n} A_{it-1} + X_o \qquad [3.13]$$

Substituting [3.10] into [3.11] yields the n reduced form asset demand equations for estimation:

$$\Delta A_i = \sum_{k=0}^{m-1} \alpha_{ik} X_k - \sum_{j=1}^{n} \gamma_{ij} A_{jt-1} \qquad [3.14]$$

The (n+1) equations [3.12] and [3.14] represent the complete model to be estimated. The following consistency conditions apply:

$$b_o + \sum_{i=1}^{n} \alpha_{io} = 1 \qquad \text{(since } X_o \text{ is income)}$$

$$b_k + \sum_{i=1}^{n} \alpha_{ik} = 0 \qquad \text{for } k = 1 \text{ to } m\text{-}1$$

$$e_j - \sum_{i=1}^{n} \gamma_{ij} = 0 \qquad \text{for } j = 1 \text{ to } n$$

These consistency conditions ensure that the budget constraint is always satisfied. Note that current wealth (X_m) does not appear in the determination of desired asset demands (unlike in the Brainard - Tobin specification [3.3]) as Purvis argues that it is the composition of wealth and not the level that determine the long run paths of consumption and portfolio decisions.

Owen (1981), following a suggestion by Smith (1978), generalises the models of Purvis and Brainard-Tobin. This general model includes end of period wealth (X_m) as an explanatory variable (X_k) to allow for sequencing effects. These are effects which relate to those variables which influence the consumption - savings decision directly but which only influence portfolio behaviour indirectly through their influence on total wealth. End of period wealth is thus treated as explicitly endogenous. However as Anderson (1984) points out it is not possible to include both income and end of period wealth simultaneously in the consumption and portfolio demand equations as the resulting system is overdetermined.

Backus and Purvis (1980) and Owen (1983a) have estimated a version of the model described by equations [3.9] and [3.11] for the US household sector and the UK personal sector respectively. Owen (1983b.) has also attempted to estimate the overdetermined integrated model described above, for the UK personal sector. The Backus and Purvis (1980) and Owen (1983a) studies both support the use of an integrated model. In particular they found that dis-aggregation of wealth improved estimates of consumption expenditures. However a major problem highlighted by these studies and Brainard - Tobin type studies of portfolio behaviour, such as those of Backus et al (1980) and Green (1982) mentioned earlier, is that models based on the multivariate stock adjustment framework have a large number of unconstrained parameters to estimate. The result is a substantial proportion of the estimates are characterised by statistical imprecision[7]. The source of the problem is the multicollinearity between the explanatory variables. Using the Friedman optimal marginal adjustment model exacerbates this problem as the α_{it}^{*} terms have to estimated thus involving a larger number of coefficients and hence greater potential for multicollinearity.

This problem of multicollinearity can be addressed in two ways. First, if the multivariate stock adjustment model is to be used then those variables with coefficients which are found to be incorrectly signed or statistically insignificant may be excluded. The model would then require re-estimation with the adding up constraints imposed. The main objections to this "data mining" approach are that the underlying model does not provide an efficient framework for imposing restrictions and that 'data mining' is an inefficient method for applying a priori information. In response to the second criticism in particular, Backus and Purvis (1980), Backus, Brainard et al (1980) and Smith and Brainard (1976),(1982) adopt the approach of explicitly incorporating personal prior information into the estimation procedure[8]. The results of these studies however were not very encouraging. Most of the statistical imprecision is removed but wrong signed parameters persisted. The cost of this approach is that the resulting coefficient estimates are subjective.

The second approach is to choose a functional form that conserves degrees of freedom and provides a more efficient framework for restrictions to be imposed. This has been the approach adopted with models of consumer demand systems, where restrictions derived from the underlying utility theory, in particular homogeneity and symmetry of prices, have been imposed in estimation.

These restrictions, if accepted by the data, reduce the number of parameters to estimate[9]. Acceptance of these restrictions is therefore particularly useful when estimating a system of asset demand equations where there are large numbers of parameters to estimate and hence a greater potential for multicollinearity. Homogeneity of interest rates implies that a change in all interest rates that leaves relative rates unchanged does not affect the demand for an asset. This restriction therefore requires that the coefficients on the interest rates in a demand equation sum to zero. Symmetry is a stronger restriction than homogeneity and implies symmetric behaviour in response to interest rates. Thus, for example, the response to a change in the interest rate on bank time deposits for the demand for building society deposits will be the same as the response to a change in the rate of interest on building society deposits for the demand for bank time deposits.

One example of a flexible functional form is the linear expenditure system (LES), applied by Saito (1977) to US household sector flow of funds. Another example is the Almost Ideal Demand System (AIDS) developed by Deaton and Muellbauer (1980b), who suggest that it possesses statistical properties superior to the LES. Demand systems, such as LES and AIDS, have the advantage that they are consistent with utility maximisation. This is not true of models based on the Brainard - Tobin approach.[10]

The AIDS asset demand equation is derived not through the more usual approach of maximising utility subject to some budget constraint but from the equivalent dual approach of minimising cost to achieve a given level of utility. This has a number of advantages including that the problem is more mathematically tractable and that it can be stated without resort to the underlying utility function. The resulting AIDS asset demand equation is specified as follows:

$$w_i = \alpha_i + \sum_j \gamma_{ij} \log p_j + \beta_i \log (W/P) \qquad [3.15]$$

where w_i = share of asset i in the portfolio
W = total sum to be allocated
p_j = price of asset j
P = price index, defined as:

$$\log P = \alpha_o + \sum_i \alpha_i \log p_i + \tfrac{1}{2} \sum\sum_{ij} \gamma_{ij} \log p_j \log p_i \qquad [3.16]$$

The following restrictions derived from utility maximisation apply to the parameters of the AIDS system :

[a] $\sum_i \alpha_i = 1$ $\sum_i \beta_i = 0$ $\sum_i \gamma_{ij} = 0$

[b] $\sum_j \gamma_{ij} = 0$

[c] $\gamma_{ij} = \gamma_{ji}$

The set of conditions [a] represent the adding up constraint. Condition [b] shows that demands are homogeneous of degree zero in prices and total expenditure. Condition [c] implies symmetry of price (p_j) coefficients[11].

If P is approximated by making it proportional to some known price index P^* then the AIDS estimating equation is as in [3.15] (i.e. no need to substitute for log P). This procedure is particularly satisfactory where prices are co-linear (e.g. interest rates).

Taylor and Clements (1983) apply a model very similar to the AIDS to Australian data for four financial assets. By imposing suitable restrictions they found the interest rate coefficients were estimated precisely.

The major limitation of the AIDS model as formulated by Deaton and Muellbauer and presented in equation [3.15] is that it assumes instantaneous adjustment to any new long run equilibrium position. As discussed earlier, the presence of adjustment costs make it unlikely that economic agents will adjust to desired long run positions in every time period. Weale (1985), (1986) presents an AIDS model incorporating dynamics within the framework of utility maximisation. The dynamics are those of myopic optimisation, that is, where economic agents do not take account of their behaviour today on their utility tomorrow. This argues Weale, can be interpreted as habit formation in the utility function underlying the model. The dynamic AIDS proposed by Weale is represented by:[12]

$$w_{it} = \alpha_i + W_t/W_{t-1} \sum_j \partial_{ij} \, w_{jt-1} \, (\log p_{jt} - \log p_{jt-1} + 1)$$

$$+ \beta_i \log (W_t/P_t) + \sum_j \gamma_{ij} \log p_j \qquad [3.17]$$

$$\text{where } W_{jt-1} = \text{lagged asset holding}$$
$$P_{jt-1} = \text{lagged price of } j^{th} \text{ asset}$$

Thus it can be seen that the asset share w_{it} in equation [3.17] is dependent on both its own lagged asset share and the lagged shares of other assets in the portfolio. Thus the interdependency in adjustment stressed in the multivariate stock adjustment model is also a feature of this dynamic AIDS model.

For short term assets where price is derived as a three month discount factor, the second term of equation [3.17] is simply:

$$\sum_j \partial_{ij} \, w_{jt-1}/W_t \qquad [3.18]$$

as the asset is not subject to revaluations. The adding up constraint:

$$\sum \partial_{ij} = 0$$

is imposed in estimation.

Weale (1986) applied the dynamic AIDS model, just described, to UK personal sector short term asset holdings. By imposing homogeneity and symmetry restrictions well determined parameter estimates were obtained. However Anderson and Blundell (1982, 1983, 1984) investigate various dynamic specifications of AIDS for disaggregated consumers expenditure and conclude that popular dynamic forms such as habit formation tend to be rejected by the data, when tested against more general specifications.

The application of symmetry and other restrictions is widespread in the consumer demand literature and increasingly so in empirical studies of portfolio behaviour. Whilst the attractions of such restrictions are clear from the earlier discussion some theoretical studies of the symmetry restriction have suggested caution about their use. Diewert (1977) shows that in general, aggregate demand functions need not satisfy any restrictions (other than those of adding up) if the number of consumers is greater than the number of goods. In portfolio studies Dalal (1983) has shown that starting from a more general utility function than the quadratic utility function, the effects of changes in expected rates of return can be decomposed into identifiable substitution and wealth effects. In a framework where substitution effects are defined as the result of changing a parameter when expected utility is held constant by adjusting initial wealth, the substitution effects are symmetric for changes in expected returns for risky assets. However, where there are both risky and secure assets in the demand system then cross substitution effects are not in general symmetric. Roley (1983) argues that a system of financial asset demands with a symmetric coefficient coefficient matrix implies that investors exhibit constant mean-variance risk aversion. Thus symmetry is not a general implication of utility maximisation but is related to the form of the individual utility functions. Further, in empirical studies of both asset demands and disaggregated consumption demands, the symmetry restriction has tended to be rejected by the data. For example, Deaton and Muellbauer (1980b) found symmetry rejected in their application of the non-dynamic AIDS model to UK consumption demands. Also, Roley (1983) tested the symmetry restriction in the context of a dis-aggregated system of demands for US Treasury securities, and found it to be rejected at low significance levels. However, Anderson and Blundell (1983) argue that the symmetry restriction is being rejected in such applications because of dynamic mis-specification and they argue for more general dynamic specification of demand systems, which can then be tested down to yield the most appropriate specification, before testing whether restrictions such as symmetry hold. Following the lesson of Anderson and Blundell, Hood (1987) developed a general dynamic system (derived from minimising the cost function described by [3.8]) of Personal Sector liquid asset demand equations and found the restrictions of symmetry and homogeneity to hold. Barr and Cuthbertson (1988), (1989) adopt the AIDS model for modelling Personal Sector liquid asset demands. They also introduce a general form of dynamics which they reparametise as an error feedback system of equations. They also adopt the Granger-Engle two step approach to estimation (discussed further in chapter 6, section 4) whereby the dynamic equations are modelled with the long run parameters held constant. This allows them to impose symmetry on the long run and dynamic parameters and they find the restrictions to hold in both cases.

3.5 Choice of model specification for this study and conclusion

In the survey of the literature discussed in this chapter two broad approaches to the modelling of consumption and portfolio behaviour of households have been identified. The first adopts the simplifying assumption of separability of preferences and therefore allows the modelling of consumption separately from asset demands. The second is the integrated approach which allows for simultaneous interrelationships between real and financial decisions. In the discussion of the separable consumption function approach it was argued that recent empirical work has increasingly recognised the role of wealth and the determinants of portfolio decisions on consumption behaviour. However this approach still falls short of allowing for the interdependent nature of portfolio and expenditure decisions. It is the integrated approach which forms the basis of this research. Two main specifications of functional form were identified for modelling a system of demands equations. These are the 'eclectic' Brainard - Tobin type model which is only loosely based on an underlying utility function and a dynamic version of the Almost Ideal Demand System (AIDS) which is explicitly derived from a utility function. Both these frameworks are general equilibrium frameworks. It was shown that a major drawback of adopting the general equilibrium approach to modelling systems of demand equations is the great potential for multicollinearity resulting from the number of free coefficients to estimate. However recent work on modelling systems of asset demands has shown that imposing restrictions such as homogeneity and symmetry can yield more plausible and significant parameters. Therefore following the work of Anderson and Blundell, for such restrictions to be accepted by the data a more general dynamic system of equations needs to specified. This will be the approach adopted in this study. It was also argued in this chapter that the AIDS model provided a more appropriate framework to facilitate the imposition of homogeneity and symmetry restrictions. However one feature of the AIDS model is that the dependent variables are shares. This poses certain problems when modelling consumption and asset demands in an integrated framework. In such a model the denominator of the shares is the sum of the dependent variables, that is, consumption plus wealth. The use of such a denominator makes the resulting shares difficult to interpret. Also attempts by this author to estimate a system of consumption and asset shares with this denominator resulted in poor fitting equations. Therefore in this research consumption and asset demands are specified in levels thereby ruling out the AIDS model. Thus a framework based on the eclectic Brainard-Tobin approach will be adopted and the actual specification adopted and the search procedure used to obtain a parsimonious system of equations is discussed in detail in chapter 6.

Notes

1. This is part of a larger model of Personal Sector behaviour a version of which has been incorporated into the main Bank of England macroeconomic model. The latest version of the Bank of England model is presented in Patterson et al (1987).

2. Income is again adjusted for inflation losses on net liquid assets.

3. Recent work by M J Dicks (1988) updates the work of Davis and in particular finds a role for interest rates in explaining both consumer durable and consumer non-durable expenditure. Dicks also uses recursive least squares on the model to examine the stability of the parameters over time and finds that interest rates effects have become more important since greater competition was introduced into the financial markets as a result of deregulation in the early 1980's.

4. In models of portfolio behaviour, liabilities are generally treated as negative assets.

5. Given the general equilibrium framework, following from Walras law, for n markets, only n-1 are estimated. The estimation results are invariant of the equation dropped - see Anderson and Blundell (1982).

6. This is equivalent to using the substitution:

$$\Delta W = \sum_j (A_j^* - A_{jt-1})$$

7. For example : Owen (1983a) - of 208 estimated coefficients, 43 were significant at the 5% level and 58 at 10%

    Backus-Purvis (1980) - of 162 estimated coefficients, 55 were significant at the 5% level.

8. Classical Mixed Estimation was used which combines subjective beliefs about the parameters together with information in the data. Prior values have to be provided for the means of all parameters in the model, together with their prior variances and covariances. The latter in particular are difficult to determine and they "..put a great strain on our intuition" (Smith and Brainard, 1976).

9. The symmetry restriction, also known as the slutsky condition, is a powerful restriction derived from utility theory (though not a necessary condition for utility maximisation behaviour). The condition implies that one half of the non-diagonal elements of the matrix of interest rate coefficients have identical components. This eliminates $(x^2 - x)/2$ independent variables from estimation: where x = number of interest rates = number of equations in system.

10. Stone (1954) has shown that all demand models which are linear in prices and consistent with utility maximisation must be derived from the Stone - Geary function underpinning the Linear Expenditure System.

11. Conditions [b] and [c] are not assumed but can be conveniently tested for.

12. To see how this is derived then, starting with the AIDS static share equation [3.15] this can be turned into an asset demand equation by multiplying through by W_t:

$$W_t w_{it} = \alpha_i W_t + W_t \beta_i \; \log(W_t/P_t)$$
$$+ \; \Sigma_j W_t \, \gamma_{ij} \; \log \; p_{jt} \qquad\qquad [3.15a]$$

Assuming myopic (habit persistence) optimisation then dynamic adjustment is incorporated by adding a lagged asset term to [3.15a]. The lagged asset holding is given by $W_{t-1} w_{it-1}$ (where w_i is the share of the asset in wealth). Now this lagged asset holding has price p_{it-1} and if subject to price revaluation over t the lagged asset holding will be revalued to $w_{it-1} W_{t-1} \cdot p_{it}/p_{it-1}$. Therefore incorporating lags into [3.15a]:

$$W_t w_{it} = \alpha_i W_t + W_{t-1} \Sigma_j \partial_{ij} \; w_{jt-1} \cdot p_{jt}/p_{jt-1}$$
$$+ \; W_t \beta_i \; \log(W_t/P_t) + \Sigma_j W_t \, \gamma_{ij} \; \log \; p_{jt} \quad [3.15b]$$

Dividing [3.15b] by W_t to obtain a share equation again we obtain:

$$w_{it} = \alpha_i + W_{t-1}/W_t \Sigma_j \partial_{ij} \; w_{jt-1} \cdot p_{jt}/p_{jt-1}$$
$$+ \; \beta_i \; \log(W_t/P_t) + \Sigma_j \gamma_{ij} \; \log \; p_{jt} \qquad [3.15c]$$

Now p_{jt}/p_{jt-1} can be approximated by:

$$(\log \; p_{jt} - \log \; p_{jt-1} + 1)$$

and substituting this in [3.15c] yields equation [3.17] in the main text.

Note that for short term assets not subject to revaluation then the dynamic version of AIDS is given by :

$$w_{it} = \alpha_i + \sum_j \partial_{ij} w_{jt-1} + \beta_i \log(W_t/P_t)$$

$$+ \sum_j \gamma_{ij} \log p_{jt} \qquad [3.17a]$$

4 Issues in constructing the data set

4.1 Introduction

Theories of asset accumulation and expenditure behaviour, outlined in chapter two, are discussed in terms of individuals or households. However published data which relates solely to households is not always available. The first part of this chapter therefore examines the problems involved in constructing a data set for estimation of the proposed model, which approaches as far as is practicable the ideal data set for the task. A related topic which is the scope of the model in terms of the portfolio decisions explained or excluded from the model is also considered. Finally the effects of inflation on asset accumulation decisions and the implications of this for the data set is discussed.

4.2 Personal sector data and its relationship to households

Most of the research into the behaviour of households

has used data relating to the Personal Sector. A useful starting point in the search for an ideal data set to model household behaviour is therefore to examine the composition of the Personal Sector as defined by the Central Statistical Office (C.S.O.).

The Personal Sector is made up of mainly households and individuals living in hostels and other institutions. However it also includes unincorporated businesses (eg. farms and the businesses of the Professions), private non-profit making bodies serving persons, NPBSP, (eg. charities, Universities and Trade Unions), the funds of life assurance and superannuation schemes (LASS), and private trusts. Work by the C.S.O. (see Jones, 1981) allows an examination of the relative importance of these sub-sectors in the various transactions reported for the Personal Sector. Table 4.1, below, shows income and expenditure in 1980 for the different sub-sectors making up the personal sector.

Table 4.1

Personal sector income and expenditure for 1980 broken down into sub-sectors

	Disposable Income	Expenditure
Households	147,863	137,135
Unincorp. Bus.	18,394	15,875
NPBSP	5,715	5,432
LASS	23,535	12,422

Note: The columns will not add to the equivalent personal sector items for 1980 because of the rearrangement of items between income and expenditure and the exclusion of intra-sector items in the personal sector account.

Source: Jones (1981)

The definition of the Household sector used by Jones includes individuals living in hostels and other institutions and private trusts as well as households. The major difference between the income of the Household sector and the Personal sector arises from the treatment of the LASS sub-sector. In the Personal sector, which includes LASS, payments to and from households by the LASS are "netted out". Thus to arrive at a definition of Household sector income, employers contributions to LASS and the investment income of the schemes are excluded, pensions and other benefits are added and employees contributions are treated as a deduction. A second adjustment made is the deduction from unincorporated business income, of estimates for stock appreciation, capital consumption and interest payments. This yields a notional household income figure representing the withdrawal of money from the business for personal use. Table 4.2 below illustrates the relationship between Household sector income and Personal sector income over the period 1975 to 1987.

Table 4.2
Ratio of household sector disposable income to personal sector disposable income (%)

1975	1976	1977	1978	1979	1980	1981
91.5	90.9	90.7	90.6	90.3	91.1	90.9

1982	1983	1984	1985	1986	1987
91.5	90.7	91.3	93.0	94.5	95.1

Source : Blue book 1989

The figures in Table 4.2 show the ratio of Household disposable income to Personal disposable income to be stable over the last half of the 1970's and early 1980's and then to rise from the mid 1980's. This is mainly due to the large increases in pensions and life assurance benefits paid net of employees contributions which were not matched by employers contributions and investment income of the schemes.

Ideally data relating to household expenditure and financial decisions should be used in estimating a model of household behaviour. Unfortunately the published data for the household sector do not, at the time of writing, include long runs of data on a quarterly basis for financial assets and liabilities. This clearly poses problem as the relationship between personal sector and household sector data varies over the period of interest for this study as evidenced by the figures for income shown in table 4.2. However this problem is mitigated to some extent by the construction of the model in this study. The proposed model is of consumption expenditure and financial and physical asset demands. It is an allocation model with essentially income being the item being allocated in the dynamic model (see chapter 6). Income in the model is constructed as the sum of the transactions in physical and financial assets less the transactions in financial liabilities plus consumption expenditure. By eliminating where identifiable those transactions which are non-household, then the income variable in the model will be closer to the household construction of income.

The C.S.O. published estimates of Personal and Household disposable income (used in table 4.2) are obtained by estimation and aggregation of a number of components such as income from employment, rent, dividends and net interest. The alternative method of obtaining a measure of income, outlined above, is to work backwards from financial and capital account transactions. Thus for 1987:

Table 4.3
Income, capital and financial transactions
of the Personal Sector (in £bn)

	Identified financial transactions (net increase in financial assets less net increase in borrowing)	15.0
+	Unidentified transactions	-21.6
+	Identified capital transactions (increase in fixed assets and stocks plus net capital transfers)	21.1
	= Saving	14.4
+	Consumers expenditure	258.4
	= INCOME	272.8

Source : Economic Trends, 1989

In theory, directly measured income should equal the definition of income obtained from the financial and capital accounts. In practice however these two constructions of income produce different results and the difference between them is reconciled by the item of unidentified transactions (often called the balancing item). The unidentified transactions item is, by convention, included in the financial transactions account but may represent mismeasurement in any or all of the financial, capital and income accounts. Recent work by the C.S.O. (reported in Economic Trends 1989) which attempts to balance these three accounts (ie. account for the unidentified transactions) for 1985/6/7 suggests mismeasurement in both the income and financial accounts. Briefly the balancing technique used by the C.S.O. involves the application of a constrained least squares method which minimises the weighted sum of squares of the differences between published and balanced values. The technique uses information on the reliabilities of the published figures, provided by the compilers of those figures. These reliability assessments and hence the final balanced figures are therefore subjective. However the resulting balanced figures for the Personal sector appear plausible. The main changes to the 1987 figures are shown in the first column of table 4.4 (ie. differences = difference between original and balanced) together with the final balanced figures :

Table 4.4
Balancing the personal sector income, capital and financial transaction accounts: 1987

	Differences	Balanced
Financial transactions	-16.2	-1.2
Unidentified transactions	21.7	0.0
Capital transactions	0.0	21.1
Saving	5.5	19.9
Consumption	-0.2	258.6
Disposable income	5.7	278.5

Source : Economic Trends, February 1989

Therefore, whilst bearing in mind the subjective nature of these adjustments, it may be judged that the published figure for income appears to be understated (perhaps reflecting the black economy) and financial transactions are overstated. The main adjustment to financial transactions is in the item transactions in UK and overseas company securities and unit trusts (£11.1bn adjustment to the original figure of £5.5bn), with smaller adjustments to other domestic transactions - which includes items like trade credit - (£4.0bn) and bank lending (£1.1bn). This reflects the unreliability of personal sector securities transactions data (calculated as a residual after allocation of transactions in this item to other sectors). These results therefore reinforce the view that personal sector income data is unreliable and hence support the construction of an income variable from financial and capital account transactions (ie. the method essentially adopted in this study). This support though is diminished by the extent of the unreliability of some financial transactions data. This clearly has implications for the choice of assets to be included in the model. Indeed, because of the unreliability of the data and for other reasons described in section 4.3.3, the assets of trade credit and company securities are excluded from the model.

4.3 Scope of the model

In this section the main issue considered is the scope of the model in terms of (i) the assets included in the model and (ii) the degree of aggregation of the included assets. The discussion is separated into four parts with the degree of aggregation of financial assets considered in 4.3.1 and a discussion of the reasons for excluding certain financial assets in 4.3.2. Section 4.3.3 examines issues relating to modelling financial liabilities whilst section 4.3.4 considers physical assets.

4.3.1 Aggregation of financial assets

Households transact in a wide range of financial instruments. The CSO financial transactions account for the Personal Sector identifies 28 financial instruments and many of these are aggregate instruments. In order to keep the modelling of transactions in financial instruments to manageable proportions further aggregation is required.

The main factor determining the aggregation was the degree of substitutability. Where instruments can be considered close substitutes, they can reasonably be combined into an aggregate instrument. Instruments can be considered as substitutes where they have similar characteristics. Given the importance of adjustment costs as a reason for integrated behaviour (discussed in chapter 2) then this is clearly an important characteristic in distinguishing the extent of substitutability between different financial instruments. Adjustment costs include information gathering costs (so the more complex an instrument, eg. equities and bonds, the higher this cost) and both pecuniary and non-pecuniary transactions costs. The life cycle hypothesis outlined in chapter two states that households desire to maintain a different time profile for expenditures from that followed by income. Financial instruments (and physical assets) can be seen as acting as buffer stocks facilitating this desire. There are two elements to this buffer stock role of asset accumulation. Firstly the desire to maintain the desired consumption pattern over the different stages of the life cycle. This involves long term decision making and tends to gives rise to transactions in assets characterised by relatively high adjustment costs such as housing and pensions. Secondly short term variability in income flows is facilitated by transactions in assets involving relatively low adjustment costs such as bank or building society deposits. It is this second role viewing the role of money or more generally liquid assets as a buffer stock which is to be found in recent literature (see Laidler (1983), Goodhart (1982) and Currie and Kenally (1985)).

Therefore a consideration of costs of adjustments leads to a distinction between liquid assets with low costs of adjustment and illiquid assets. The category of liquid assets can be further separated, by reference again to the characteristic of associated adjustment costs, into money and its close substitutes like sight deposits on the one hand and the rest of liquid assets on the other. In this study a further separation of the other liquid assets category into bank time deposits, building society deposits and national savings instruments is made on the grounds of the greater scope provided for simulation experiments with the model. The only illiquid financial asset category modelled in this research is public sector debt. Other illiquid financial assets held by the Personal Sector are excluded for reasons discussed in section 4.3.2. Table 4.5 below provides a classification of the aggregate financial assets modelled in this study and this is followed by a more detailed discussion of the various categories.

Table 4.5
Financial assets included in the model

Aggregate financial instrument	Components
1. Transaction balances (TRS)	- Notes and Coin - Sterling sight deposits - NS Ordinary Account
2. Bank time deposits (BTD)	- Sterling bank time deposits
3. Building Society ordinary shares and deposits (BSD)	- Building Society shares and deposits (excl. SAYE)
4. National Savings instruments (NATSAV)	- NS Investment Account - NS Certificates (conventional ie. excl. Index linked and SAYE) - NS Stamps, Gift Tokens, Savings Bonds (excl. premium bonds)
5. Public Sector debt (PSD)	- Local Authority listed securities, bonds - British Govt. securities - Other Govt. guaranteed securities - Temporary Deposits with Local Authorities

Asset category 1 (TRS) is comprised of instruments with very low adjustment costs, held mainly for transaction purposes. The majority of the components of this asset had until recently no associated explicit interest rate. Bank sight deposits carried a notional rate of interest which could be offset against bank charges over some of the period of investigation. Grice et al (1981) noted however that much of this interest is dissipated and thus the notional interest rate is ignored. There is an explicit interest rate on overnight (wholesale) sight deposits and on National Savings (NS) Ordinary Accounts. However, for the former, no data on the size of such deposits exists for the Personal Sector although it is thought that the size will be low compared to the total for this aggregate. For the latter, the interest rate has always been low (say, compared to interest rates in asset category 2) and the proportion of this component to the total aggregate is low. Interest bearing chequeing accounts started to appear in 1983 and have grown significantly as a proportion of sight deposits since that time. This clearly needs to be allowed for in modelling. One approach (see Barr and Cuthbertson, (1989)) is to use a time trend, starting in 1983, to capture the "learning" process as agents in the Personal Sector adjust to the innovation. However it is assumed that there is no explicit interest rate for this category.

Asset categories 2 (BTD) and 3 (BSD) are interest bearing deposits. Some sterling time deposits are of a longer term than the average term for this category but as with sight deposits no data showing the breakdown by term exists for the Personal Sector. Despite the similar characteristics for these two assets they are included separately in the model to investigate the competition between the two issuing institutions over the period covered by the research. The respective interest rates are the 7 day Clearing Bank deposit rate (adjusted for tax at the standard rate - see below) for BTD and the rate on building society ordinary shares for BSD. With regard to the rate on building society ordinary shares and deposits reported by the Building Societies Association, this basic rate has become increasingly less representative of interest paid on typical building society shares since premium accounts were introduced in 1980. Thus from 1980 an average rate paid on building society shares is used (prior to 1980 there is little difference between the basic and average rate).

Asset category 4 (NATSAV) consists of various National Savings instruments with different characteristics. For example the National Savings investment account has a shorter average term than National Savings certificates where the certificates have to be held for at least 3 years to gain the full benefits. The reason why these instruments are included together is that they are issued by the same institution which is effectively under the instructions of HM Treasury. When there is a greater requirement for Government funding through the medium of National Savings then often the terms and conditions on the different National Savings instruments are adjusted at the same time. The return on NATSAV is a weighted average of the returns on the two main components, that is, the rate of interest on National Savings investment account (adjusted for tax) and the rate of interest on the prevailing National Savings fixed interest certificate. The weights used are end of period stocks of the component assets.

Asset 5 (PSD) are Government securities with a term to maturity of greater than one year. The capital uncertain characteristic of government securities implies that expectations of capital gain/loss will play a role in demand. In order to simplify the modelling of expectations the assumption is made that investors have a one period (ie one quarter in this research) holding period and therefore only one period ahead expectations of capital gain need to be considered. At time t-1, actual one period ahead capital gain, CGt, is given by :

$$CG_t = (P_t - P_{t-1})/P_{t-1} \qquad [4.1]$$

There is a problem with modelling expectations of capital gains in that the variable defined by [4.1] will be characterised by high frequency due to quarterly movements in the price of government securities. It can be argued (see Currie and Kenally, (1985)) that the decision to move into this high adjustment cost asset will generally be for a long period. Thus agents will look beyond the high frequency to the underlying rate of return. Thus expected capital gains are modelled using a four quarter moving average to smooth out the high frequency :

$$E_{t-1}CG_t = 1/4 \ E_{t-1}(CG_t + CG_{t-1} + CG_{t-2} + CG_{t-3}) \quad [4.2]$$

The McCallum (1976) technique is used to model expected capital gains as defined by [4.2] and the results of this are presented in Appendix 4A. The full return on government securities is then given by the running yield (taken as the redemption yield on medium term government securities) plus expected capital gain.

Turning now to general issues about interest rates, some of those used in the model are post tax (eg. building society deposit rate) whilst some are pre tax (eg. bank time deposit rate over the estimation period) with tax paid at the end of the tax year by taxpayers. To overcome the problems posed by these different tax effects the interest rates are standardised by assuming that all interest is taxed at the standard rate. Thus interest rates quoted pre tax are adjusted for tax at the standard rate. It is further assumed that capital gains are untaxed which is probably a reasonable assumption given the high tax threshold for capital gains tax and that capital gains are tax exempt on government bonds held for longer than 12 months.

There is also a potential estimation problem resulting from possible endogeneity of interest rate terms. The personal sector are principle holders of building society deposits and national savings and major holders of bank deposits. It is clearly beyond the scope of this research to develop models of bank and building society behaviour to model the supply side. One possible solution is to use an instrumental variables technique such as three stage least squares when estimating the model. However it is thought that the problem of endogeneity is not likely to be severe as the interest rate data is quarterly averaged whereas the portfolio data is end of quarter.

Thus interest rates can be seen as largely pre-determined in the model.

4.3.2 Liabilities

Households issue essentially two main categories of liabilities, each used to finance different types of asset purchases. These two categories are loans to finance house purchase and unsecured consumer credit used to finance the purchase of consumer durables and to a lesser extent consumer non-durables. Both these categories of liabilities are included separately in the model and their construction and corresponding own rates of interest are shown in table 4.6.

Table 4.6
Liabilities included in the model

Loans for house purchase (LHP)	BSA Mortgage
- Banks	rate (RLHP)
- Public Sector	
- Other Financial Institutions	

Consumer Credit (CONCR)	Bank base rate
- Sterling Bank lending (other than for house purchase)	plus 12% (RCONCR)
- Hire Purchase and other Instalment Debt	

RLHP is adjusted for the standard rate of income tax to reflect the actual rate paid by households. It needs to be noted though that as tax relief is calculated using the marginal tax rate then the tax adjusted rate does not reflect the actual interest charges for those borrowers paying more than the standard rate. However it will reflect the interest charges for the majority of borrowers Also, tax relief is only allowed up to some maximum set by the Government (presently £30,000) and the rapid growth of house prices in the 1980's has pushed up the average price and hence the average new mortgage advance above the limit for tax relief (since 1987). This is not a serious problem at present as the average mortgage outstanding is still less than the limit set for tax relief.

RCONCR is not adjusted for tax. The 12% addition to base rate is used to reflect the average interest charges on unsecured borrowing by households.

There are problems with estimating the effects of the own interest rate on these two types of borrowing over the estimation period (1976 to 1987) as for parts of this period there were restrictions on borrowing. These restrictions will now be considered along with other institutional developments in the markets for mortgages and consumer credit.

4.3.2.1 Loans for house purchase (mortgages) Over the 1970's the building societies dominated the mortgage market and there was very little competition from banks on this front as the banks were restricted by the imposition of direct controls on their lending, which impinged most directly on the personal sector. Building societies were not profit maximisers but attempted to reconcile the conflicting demands of borrowers for low rates of interest and savers for high rates by maintaining a relatively stable path for interest rates over time. This was made possible by the cartel arrangement which existed whereby the Building Societies Association (BSA) recommended rates of interest to be charged to savers and borrowers. Such an institutional structure minimised the role played by interest rates in equilibriating supply and demand for mortgages. The stickiness of interest rates offered by building societies on shares and deposits meant that at times the rates offered were uncompetitive thus reducing inflows. This shortage of funds for lending that occurred at times could be made up by running down liquid assets. However this provided only a temporary solution and given that societies would not raise interest rates to reduce demand for mortgages accordingly, then other means of rationing were pursued. These included queues and changes in lending arrangements - for example lowering the ratios of loans to borrowers income or the value (price) of associated property.

The market structure just described began to break down shortly after the start of the 1980's decade. In mid 1980 direct controls on bank lending (the Corset) were lifted and the banks immediately strove to develop areas of business where they had previously had little activity. In particular they entered the mortgage market and by 1982 they had achieved a market share of new lending in excess of 40%. From 1983 bank mortgage lending grew more slowly, in part because their initial targets had been met. After mid 1985 the banks again targeted the personal sector, partly because of increased risks associated with foreign lending and partly because of the increasing use of the securities markets by large companies (the growing phenomenon of dis-intermediation). Thus the banks share of new mortgage lending again increased. Also since the mid 1980's a number of new lending institutions have entered the mortgage market including foreign banks and non-banks financing lending through funds borrowed from the wholesale markets. Thus competition in the mortgage market has grown more intense over the 1980's.

The greater competition in both mortgage and retail deposit markets led to a shift in building society behaviour. In particular the societies became more sensitive to interest rate changes and as a consequence the cartel arrangement broke down following the withdrawal of one of the largest societies (Abbey National) in 1982. Another change in building societies behaviour followed from allowing societies entry into the wholesale money and capital markets. In 1983 they began to issue wholesale time deposits and CD's and in 1985 they made their first issues in the eurosterling market. Receipts from these activities accounted for approximately one third of all inflows in 1986. Use of the wholesale markets has allowed societies to practice liability management in order to fully fund the demand for mortgages. Thus the direction of causation between inflows and lending has to some extent been reversed over the 1980's.

The 1980's has therefore seen greater competition in the mortgage market and as a consequence a greater availability of mortgage funds leading to a growth in mortgage lending. As described above though, there have been times over the period from 1970 to the present when the mortgage market was characterised by rationing. Empirical research to support this is provided by Pratt (1980), Anderson and Hendry (1984), Wilcox (1985) and Hall and Urwin (1989). The observed institutional structure, described above, also lends weight to the proposition of rationed mortgages. During times of rationing the demand for mortgages is less likely to be influenced by the rate of interest charged. However identifying the periods when significant mortgage rationing took place is not straightforward. Both Wilcox (1985) and Hall and Urwin (1989) using different approaches to modelling the building society sector find significant excess demand for mortgages over the period 1973 to 1975, negligible excess demand from 1976 to 1978 then significant (though less than 73-75) excess demand from 1978 to 1980. Wilcox only models up to 1983 but finds no evidence of excess demand in the period mid-1980 to 1983. Hall and Urwin find a similar result. This is not surprising as the period after mid-1980 corresponds to the aggressive entry of banks into the mortgage market following the removal of the Corset restriction. What is surprising is the result from Hall and Urwin that significant excess demand for mortgages appeared again at the end of 1983 lasting until at least the end of 1985 (the end of the estimation period for Hall and Urwin). This may reflect the slow down in bank lending in the mortgage market at this time. However the mortgage market was more competitive at that time and the building societies more flexible in interest rate setting so it is unlikely that rationing existed to the same degree as the 1970's.

What is clear from the preceding discussion is that rationing of mortgages existed for some of period covered by this study (1976 to 1987) and that this rationing was probably more pronounced over the first half of this period. In order to identify the effects of the mortgage interest rate on demand the influence of rationing needs to be allowed for. It was mentioned above that the rationing mechanisms used by building societies in the

56

1970's were the use of queues and changes in lending arrangements, notably, a decrease in the loan to house value ratio (LVR) or a decrease in the loan to borrowers income ratio (LYR). There is no long run of data on the extent of queues for mortgages but data exists for LVR and LYR. There are problems with using the published data on LYR to proxy rationing, in particular the different constructions of income used by the various building societies publishing data. Therefore following Wilcox, the LVR for first time buyers is used in this research to proxy rationing in the mortgage market.

4.3.2.2 Consumer credit Consumer credit is defined in this research as unsecured bank lending, short term loans by other financial institutions (mainly finance houses) and loans from credit companies and retailers. The stock of consumer credit in 1980's prices rose by 42% between 1976 and 1980 and by 110% over the next 7 years. Within this growth unsecured bank lending increased its share of the total, accounting for 75% of total consumer credit at the start of the period (1976) staying at roughly the same level until 1980, but increasing to 86% by 1987. As with the mortgage market the components of consumer credit were subject to restrictions over the first half of the period. These restrictions were of two types, namely controls on the balance sheet of the lending institutions (the Corset - discussed earlier) and controls on the terms and conditions of the loan. Terms controls on consumer credit operated primarily on goods obtained under hire purchase agreements. Such loans were specific to individual purchases making it easier to impose conditions on them. The conditions imposed consisted of a minimum deposit (ie. 100% loans to finance purchase were not permitted) and/or a maximum repayment period for the loan. Terms controls were in operation at the start of the period covered in this research and officially ended in July 1982. The conditions imposed varied over the period and according to the type of good being purchased. Parallel terms controls applied to personal bank loans and latterly for credit cards. These controls though were known to be "leaky" as they were less closely tied to the purchase of specific goods.

As with the modelling of the demand for mortgages, in order to identify the influence of the rate of interest on demand for consumer credit it is necessary to allow for the rationing that took place in the market. In order to capture the effects of the Corset on bank lending an on-off dummy variable was used. The Corset took the form of a requirement for non-interest bearing 'supplementary special deposits' to be made at the Bank of England by banks whose interest bearing eligible liabilities (and hence their assets) grew at above a specified rate (discussed in detail in the Bank of England Quarterly Bulletin (1982)). The Corset operated in 1977 quarter one and two and from 1978 quarter two to 1980 quarter two inclusive. The dummy variable was set to one when the Corset was in operation and zero at other times. Unfortunately, on estimation, the expected signs on this dummy variable (negative - implying less lending when the Corset was in operation) were not found in the consumer credit equation or the demand for consumer durables equation. However a simpler dummy variable which has the value zero up to and including 1980 quarter two and the value one after, designed to pick up the release of the pent up demand in the consumer credit (and mortgage) market following the removal of the Corset, was more successful having the expected signs in the consumer credit and consumer durables (and mortgage) equations. No attempt was made to capture the effects of the imposition and removal of terms controls as these controls, as described above, had only a weak effect on unsecured bank lending which accounted for three quarters of consumer credit during their imposition.

There were still problems encountered in finding a role for the rate of interest on consumer credit (RCONCR) in explaining the demand for consumer credit even after incorporating the effects of rationing. Including RCONCR in the model produced the "wrong" own sign. In order to find a role for RCONCR on the demand for consumer credit, RCONCR was set to zero for parts of the estimation period, starting with 1976 quarter 1 to 1980 quarter two (ie. the period which for some of the time was characterised by rationing - captured by the dummy variable) and then extending the period by two quarters each time. The expected sign for RCONCR in the demand for consumer credit equation was found when RCONCR was allowed to have an effect for the period after 1983 quarter three (ie. 1983 Q3 to 1987 Q4). This implies that households became sensitive to (real) interest rates on consumer credit after mid-1983. This may reflect the increasing indebtedness of households following the removal of the Corset - making them more sensitive to interest rate changes - and at the same time an upward growth in real interest rates over early 1980's. There is some supportive empirical evidence for households only becoming responsive to interest rates on consumer credit in the 1980's in work reported by Dicks (1988) in relation to modelling consumption.

4.3.3 Financial assets/liabilities excluded from the model

It should be clear from the the preceeding discussion of financial assets and liabilities included in the model that not all financial assets/liabilities held by households are covered. A major set of assets excluded from the model are UK company securities, unit trusts, and overseas securities (mainly overseas company securities) which at the end of 1987 accounted for approximately 18% of gross financial asset stocks. The share of company securities in gross financial asset stocks fell over the 1970's although this trend has been checked and possibly reversed since 1982. Although the change in the stock of this asset has always been positive, this is due to revaluations, whilst net purchases of the asset have been negative over most of the period of interest (only in 1986 did net annual transactions become positive). This represents a trend whereby the Personal Sector have moved away from direct long term investment in "risky" assets to indirect investment through Life Assurance and Superannuation Schemes. Such a trend is not easily explained in an allocation model where the main determinants of asset holdings are rates of return. Also as mentioned earlier in this chapter, the data on company securities transactions and hence holdings of this asset are particularly unreliable. Therefore UK company securities and unit trusts are not explained in the proposed model, but in order to test for the influence of wealth held in the form of equities on portfolio and consumption decisions an equity wealth variable will be included as an additional explanatory variable.

One of the most significant changes in the personal sector's balance sheet over the period covered by the analysis is the rise in the share of Life Assurance and Superannuation Schemes (LASS) holdings. This has in creased from around 26% of gross financial assets in 1975 to around 42% in 1987. Approximately 50% of the increase in the value of LASS over this period has been due to revaluations of the assets held by LASS. However, the contractual nature of employees contributions to pension funds and the weak relationship between the value of a fund and the benefits received by households in many cases (ie. most occupational pension schemes pay benefits according to number of years worked multiplied by a factor of 1/60 or 1/80 multiplied by final salary), suggests that it is households may not take account of this asset in assessing their net wealth position. Although at times of pension fund surplus (ie. expected assets > expected liabilities) such as in the early 1980's, may lead to a reduction in employee contributions and thus affect other forms of saving. For life assurance policies there is likely to be a more direct link between the value of a fund and future benefits (and thus current saving) in terms of the accrued bonus. Also, an important determinant of the rapid growth in LASS has been the favourable tax treatment - this is difficult to allow for within the context of a portfolio model. So for these reasons the asset represented by LASS will not be explained in the proposed model, but in order to test for a possible LASS wealth effect on household portfolio and expenditure decisions, the holdings of LASS will also be included as an additional explanatory variable.

Other financial assets/liabilities found in the Personal sector balance sheet but not included in the model are trade credit, tax instruments and accruals of taxes rates and interest. The first two items are excluded on the grounds that they are likely to be instruments which are mainly traded by the non-household part of the personal sector. The last item is excluded on the grounds of treating income on a cash flow rather than an accruals basis. Other financial instruments excluded from the model are not very significant.

4.3.4 Physical assets

The two physical assets explained in the model are consumer durables and dwellings. Other tangible assets appearing in the personal sector balance sheet, including plant and machinery, stocks and work in progress, are excluded on the grounds that they relate to the non-household part of the personal sector.

4.3.4.1 Consumer durables
To begin we consider the issue of whether to define consumption as total consumption expenditure (i.e. consumption of non-durables and durables) or whether the non-durable and durable components should be split and modelled separately. It is clear that demand for durables is the demand for a stock whereas demand for non-durables is a flow expenditure. However the problem with making this distinction is where to make the time period cut off between a durable and non-durable good. Items of clothing can be considered durable goods if the time period is taken to be a few weeks but a non-durable good if the time period is a year or two. The C.S.O. (see Calder (1978)) defines a consumer durable as "anything bought by consumers that lasts and provides services for longer than one year". The adoption of the one year lifetime is clearly an arbitrary definition and will therefore produce anomalies but it does allow for the treatment of those goods such as cars and electrical goods, which clearly provide a lasting service, to be treated as wealth. Thus consumer durables are modelled in this study as an

asset.

At present there exists no published quarterly series for stocks of consumer durables for the UK, although the C.S.O. has published annual estimates (Calder, 1978). The C.S.O. estimates are calculated using a perpetual inventory method developed by Stone and Rowe (1957). The estimates in Calder were calculated on three different life length assumptions (short, medium and long) for category of durable and using two methods of depreciation (straight line and reducing balance). As Calder points out the resulting stock series is very sensitive to the assumed length (and hence implied depreciation rate) and method of depreciation, although the change in the stock series is less sensitive. The C.S.O. consumer durable stock estimates reported in Reid (1978) and in subsequent Financial Statistics personal sector balance sheets are based on the assumption of medium life length and reducing balance depreciation. Therefore following Owen (1986) the quarterly equivalents of medium life length for the three durable categories of furniture and floor coverings, motor vehicles and household appliances were applied to quarterly data for expenditure on these items using the reducing balance perpetual inventory method. The resulting three series were aggregated to provide quarterly consumer durable stocks for this research.

Briefly, with the perpetual inventory reducing balance method the value of the asset stock reduces by a fixed proportion of its beginning of period value. The C.S.O. calculations make the assumption that the value of the asset, at constant prices, is reduced to 5 per cent of its original value before it is retired from the stock. It can be shown (see Owen (1986)) that the stock of consumer durables at the end of period t is given by :

$$SCD_t = (1-\partial)SCD_{t-1} + (1-\partial)^{\frac{1}{2}}CDE_t - (1-\partial)^{n+\frac{1}{2}}CDE_{t-n-1} \quad [4.3]$$

where SCD = stock of consumer durable
CDE = consumer durable expenditure
n   = life length

The depreciation rate, ∂, is found by solving:

$$(1-\partial)^{n-\frac{1}{2}} = 0.05 \quad\quad\quad [4.4]$$

The assumed life lengths and the implied depreciation rates (see table 4.7 below) are those adopted by Owen which in turn are quarterly versions of the medium life assumptions reported in appendix 2 of Calder.

Table 4.7

Expenditure category	Assumed life length (quarters)	Implied ∂ (%)
Furniture and floor coverings	92	3.22
Motor vehicles	36	8.09
Household Appliances	39	7.49

As mentioned above the dependent variable in the model will be the change in the stock of consumer durables:

$$\Delta SCD = SCD - SCD_{t-1} \quad\quad [4.5]$$

Now, using an approximate (straight line) version of [4.3] ie. :

$$SCD = (1-\partial)SCD_{t-1} + CDE \quad\quad [4.6]$$

we can see that:

$$\Delta SCD = CDE - \partial SCD_{t-1} \quad\quad [4.7]$$

Thus the dependent variable for the dynamic model

consumer durables equation when added to the other dependent variables to form the income variable, contributes to the formation of a Hicksian version of income (ie. the amount that can be spent whilst leaving the stock of wealth intact). This is because, as equation [4.7] shows, the depreciation in SCD which needs to be financed if the stock of wealth is maintained is deducted from expenditure. Thus the dependent variable is expenditure on durables after allowance for maintainance of the existing stock. This is the approach taken by Stone (1973) and more recently by Patterson (1985). Extension of this concept of Hicksian income to inflation effects on assets is covered in the next section.

There is no obvious rate of return on consumer dura bles. In the neo-classical approach to modelling the demand for consumer durables (see Deaton and Muellbauer (1980a)) it is postulated that such demand is in versely related to the user cost of durables, v^* , defined in [4.8]

$$v^* = PCD_{t-1} - PCD_t(1-\partial)/(1+r_t) \qquad [4.8]$$

where PCD = price of consumer durables
        ∂ = depreciation rate
        r = interest rate

The user cost of durables is defined as the cost of holding one unit of durables for one period. It can be seen from [4.8] that if PCD_t > PCD_{t-1} (ie. capital gains expected) then the user cost of durables will decrease and consumer durables will become more desirable. Under reasonable assumptions of ∂ and r it is possible to produce low or even negative user costs. If negative user costs result then in the neo-classical approach, demand for consumer durables becomes infinite. This is clearly unrealistic. Another major objection to this approach is that it assumes perfect capital markets which again is unrealistic when it is considered that borrowing constraints were severe over the 1970's and these affected the ability to borrow to finance consumer durable purchases in particular. However a useful result from this analysis is that expected capital gains on durables are likely to encourage consumers to bring forward purchases of durables. Therefore expected capital gains on consumer durables will be used as a proxy for the rate of return on durables in this research. The method of obtaining this variable and the implications of using it in the model are considered after the next section on modelling dwellings.

4.3.4.2 Dwellings The second tangible asset modelled in this research is owner occupied housing. The share of owner occupied in the total stock of dwellings has grown from around 50 per cent in 1970 to around 64 per cent in 1987. This growth has accelerated since 1980, in part due to the transfer of over a million council houses into private ownership since that time.

Housing is first and foremost a basic necessity but when owned by the household can also be considered as an asset which like other financial and physical assets, yields a return. The most easily identified return to housing investment is capital gain resulting from increased house prices. Over the estimation period house prices have almost consistently shown a positive nominal increase. This capital gain can be realised by "trading down" at retirement. Also housing equity can be used as collateral for borrowing and this in fact provides another way of releasing the equity. Equity withdrawal from housing by the personal sector defined as borrowing secured on property greater than that required to purchase or improve the property, exceeded £17 billion in 1987 (Barclays Bank, 1989).

As with consumer durables, the C.S.O. publish annual estimates of the stock of housing but not quarterly fig ures. In this research an attempt was made to infer a depreciation rate (to account for slum clearance etc.) for annual data, from which a quarterly depreciation rate could then be calculated. The following equation, implying straight line depreciation, was estimated :

$$DWE/PH = (1-\partial)DWE_{-1}/PH_{-1} + INVDWE/PH \qquad [4.9]$$

where   PH   = mix-adjusted price of dwellings[a]
           INVDWE= private sector investment in dwellings
           DWE   = stock of dwellings

Note a: The Department of Environment constructed house price index based on completed transactions and weighted according to the mix of dwelling types.

    Private sector investment in dwellings was used as a proxy for personal sector investment in dwellings (for which no quarterly series and only a short run of annual data is available). Private sector investment in dwellings is slightly higher than personal sector as it includes investment by the industrial and commercial companies sector. However the annual average of personal to private sector investment in dwellings for annual data has been fairly constant around 0.9 . However a depreciation rate slightly higher than one was found which clearly does not make sense as houses have a limited life (albeit a fairly long one). The problems probably lie in the data, in particular the problem of reconciling housing stock data which is calculated using rating valuation and investment in housing data which is directly measured. Therefore an approximate method of interpolation was used to obtain a quarterly stock consistent with the published C.S.O. annual stock. The following relation was used to obtain quarterly estimates:

$$DWE = DWE_{-1} + ((PH - PH_{-1})/PH_{-1})DWE_{-1}$$
$$+ INVDWE \qquad [4.10]$$

The transactions and capital gains were cumulated for each year separately and any discrepancy between the final year stock and the C.S.O. estimate is used to adjust each quarterly estimate on the basis of the pro portional investment in the quarter.

    The return on housing investment as outlined earlier,

is proxied in this research by expected capital gains on housing. Construction of such a variable will be considered in the next section.

4.3.4.3 Rate of return on physical assets As previously described the rates of return on the two physical assets are to be proxied by expected capital gains on the re spective asset. This has implications for the model which will now be discussed. In the proposed model, in order to satisfy the adding up constraint, the sum allocated which appears as a variable on the right hand side is equal to the sum of the dependent variables (ie. consumption plus physical assets plus financial assets minus financial liabilities). This allocated variable can be separated into three components :

$$\text{sum allocated} = NW_{-1} + Y + CG$$

where NW_{-1} is net wealth at the beginning of the period, Y is income and CG is capital gains accruing over the period. This capital gain component can be further split into the components of gains on dwellings (CGDWE), public sector debt (CGPSD) and consumer durables (CGCD) ie. :

$$CG = CGDWE + CGPSD + CGCD$$

These capital gains are actual capital gains which will be unknown at the time households make their allocation decisions. Also, it is expected capital gains on dwellings and consumer durables which are to be used as proxies for rates of return, therefore expected capital gains are estimated using the McCallum (1976) technique and the results are described in the appendix to this chapter. The unexpected components also need to be included in the model in order to satisfy the adding up condition. The unexpected components are simply calculated as actual minus expected capital gains.

Expected capital gains should have a positive effect on the asset to which it accrues. In addition, expected capital gain on physical assets implies that less of other forms of capital accumulation are needed to increase wealth to desired levels. Therefore expected capital gains on physical assets should have a negative effect on financial asset demands and hence a positive effect on consumption. The unexpected component of capital gains should have little effect during the period in which they accrue except for the asset to which they are accruing. This is because a response to unexpected capital gains implies that households adjust their plans during the period of accrual.

4.4 Inflation effects

Inflation has the effect of eroding the real value (purchasing power) of assets - in particular the real value of capital certain assets such as deposits. Inflation has the opposite effect on liabilities, reducing the real value of outstanding debt. It has been suggested (see for example, Taylor and Theadgold (1979), Jump (1980) and Von Ungern-Sternberg (1981)) that during times of high inflation households save more in order to maintain a real desired stock of assets. Also where high inflation leads to high nominal interest rates then saving (defined as income less consumption) is mismeasured as part of the flow of interest payments (which are part of income) are conceptually capital repayments rather than asset accu mulation. It has therefore been suggested that measured income and hence saving should be reduced by inflation losses/gains on assets/liabilities. This leads to a concept of income close to the Hicksian definition: "the maximum value which (an individual) can consume during a week, and still expect to be as well off at the end of the week as he was at the beginning", (Hicks, 1946). This inflation adjusted definition of income and hence saving is normally termed "real" to distinguish it from deflated income termed real.

The accounting relationship between income, saving, asset accumulation and inflation adjustment is illustrated in the following identity[1] :

$$Y/P - C/P = [A/P - A_{-1}/P_{-1}]$$
$$+ [(P - P_{-1})/P] * A_{-1}/P_{-1} \qquad [4.11]$$

or

DEFLATED = CHANGE IN INFLATION ADJUSTED
SAVING ASSET STOCK

   + INFLATION LOSS ON ASSET STOCK

where Y = Income
    C = Consumption
    A = Asset stock at end of period
    P = Consumer price index

Re-arranging equation [4.11] to give:

$$Y/P - C/P - [(P - P_{-1})/P] * A_{-1}/P_{-1}$$
$$= [A/P - A_{-1}/P_{-1}] \qquad [4.12]$$

ie. "Real" SAVING = CHANGE IN INFLATION ADJUSTED
       ASSET STOCK

Thus the inflation adjusted asset stock is simply the asset stock measured in constant price terms. The consumer price index is used for deflating the asset stock yielding a series measured in constant consumption terms (which appears reasonable when it is considered that according to the life cycle hypothesis consumption is the ultimate objective of asset accumulation). The change in this stock is equal to "real" saving ie. deflated saving less inflation loss on the opening asset stock.

A related issue is whether to use real or nominal rates of interest as determinants of consumption and portfolio behaviour. In a taxless world, the Fisher equation relates the real rate of interest r, the nominal rate i, and the rate of price inflation p :

$$r = (i-p)/(1+p) \qquad [4.13]$$

$(1+r)$ represents the rate at which consumers can transform current real saving into future real consumption. It was mentioned in the earlier section on asset categories that interest rates in the study have been adjusted for taxes. Introducing taxes modifies the Fisher equation to :

$$r = [(1-t)(i-p)]/(1+p) \qquad [4.14]$$

where t = proportional tax rate (assumed to be standard rate tax)

It can be shown that the adjustment of measured income for inflation erosion of net monetary assets ie. (from [4.12]) :

$$\text{"real income"} = Y/P - ((P - P_{-1})/P) * A_{-1}/P_{-1} \qquad [4.15]$$

$$\text{or "real income"} = Y/P - p * A_{-1}/P \qquad [4.16]$$

implies the replacement of the after tax interest flow in conventional measured income ie. :

$$(1-t)i * A_{-1}/P \qquad [4.17]$$

with the alternative measure :

$$(1+p)r * A_{-1}/P \qquad [4.18]$$

To see this we need to write conventional measured income in terms of its non-interest, z, and interest components ie. :

$$Y/P = z + (1-t)i * A_{-1}/P \qquad [4.19]$$

Substituting [4.19] into [4.16] we get :

$$\text{"real income"} = z + (1-t)i * A_{-1}/P - p * A_{-1}/P \qquad [4.20]$$

Now re-arranging the Fisher equation [4.14] :

$$(1+p)r + p = (1-t)i \qquad [4.21]$$

Substituting [4.21] into [4.20] gives :

"real income" $= z + (1+p)r\,A_{-1}/P$ [4.22]

Thus the inflation adjustment procedure implies that interest flows are better measured using real as opposed to nominal rates of interest. Therefore it is real interest rates that are used in this study and these are defined as in [4.14].

In economics, emphasis is generally placed upon ex pected variables, especially prices, as determinants of households behaviour. The real rate of interest formula should therefore be amended to incorporate expected inflation, $E_{t-1}p = p^e$. Thus (from eqn. [4.14]) :

$$r = [\ (1-t)i - p^e\ ]/(1+p^e)$$ [4.23]

An implication of using equation [4.23] is that the infla-tion effect on monetary assets/liabilities discussed earlier should be treated as expected inflation effects.

An expected inflation variable therefore needs to be constructed. Various techniques have been used by re searchers to obtain an expected price series. Expectations formation has been modelled using "error learning", extrapolative and rational models of behaviour. It is not always clear as to which method to choose. It is argued here that households do not use the straight rational forward looking approach when forming expectations but instead use a mixture of backward and forward looking behaviour. Therefore in this study inflation expectations are formed by using an average of the current 12 month rate and the actual rate one year ahead :

$$p^e = ((P_t/P_{t-4})-1)\ ^*\ 50 + ((P_{t+4})/P_t)-1)\ ^*\ 50$$ [4.24]

This implies knowledge on the part of agents of the personal sector of the price level one years hence. As with expected capital gains the McCallum technique is used to generate the expected price level P_{t+4} and the results of this analysis are reported in Appendix 4A. The expected inflation series is then generated using [4.24].

There is a still a problem with assuming that households know the current price level, P_t. However as with interest rates, this problem is mitigated to the extent that P_t is the average price level for the quarter and is therefore largely pre-determined.

4.5 Summary of variables in the model

4.5.1 Dependent variables

The set of dependent variables incorporates five financial asset categories, two tangible asset categories, two financial liability categories and consumption expenditures. These are all real variables (ie. deflated by the consumer price deflator) and are listed in the table below together with the variable names used in the research:

Consumption expenditures	CON
Transaction money	TRS
Bank Time Deposits	BTD
Building Society Deposits	BSD
National Savings	NATSAV
Public Sector Debt	PSD
Dwellings	DWE
Consumer Durables	CD
Loans for House Purchase	LHP
Consumer credit	CONCR

4.5.2 Explanatory variables

The main explanatory variables in the proposed model are the real rates of return on the four interest earning assets and the real interest rates on the two liabilities. As real rates of return are used then the "cost" of holding or allocating funds to transaction money, where no interest return is paid to compensate for inflation erosion of the asset stock, will be proxied by the negative of the expected inflation variable. Thus expected inflation is entered as a separate explanatory variable. The two tangible assets have no easily identifiable rates of return. The proxy variables for the rates of return on the two tangible assets are expected capital gains ie. ECGDWE and ECGCD.

Two additional explanatory variables included in the model, for reasons mentioned earlier in this chapter, are a real stock of equity wealth variable (ie. stock of equity wealth deflated by implicit consumer deflator), (EQUITY), and a real Life Assurance and Pension Fund wealth variable, (LAPF). Also, a trend (TREND) variable beginning in 1983 quarter four is included to capture the learning process after interest bearing chequeing accounts are introduced. Finally to capture rationing in the credit markets the Loan to Value ratio (LVR) is included to proxy rationing in the mortgage market and a dummy variable (DUMMY) is included to capture the explosion of demand in the consumer credit market following the removal of the Corset.

Thus the complete list of explanatory variables in the proposed model is given below :

RBTD	Real rate of interest on bank time deposits
RBSD	Real rate of interest on building society deposits
RNATSAV	Real rate of interest on national savings instruments
RPSD	Real rate of return (running yield + expected capital gain) on public sector debt
RCONCR	Real rate of interest on consumer credit
RLHP	Real rate of interest on loans for house purchase
ECGDWE	Real expected capital gains on dwellings
ECGCD	Real expected capital gains on consumer durables
P^e	Expected inflation
EQUITY	Real stock of company securities held by the Personal sector
LAPF	Real stock of equity in Life Assurance and

Pension Funds
LVR   Loan to value ratio
TREND   Trend beginning in 1983 Q4
DUMMY   Dummy variable (1976 Q1 to 1980 Q2 =0,
                           1980 Q3 to 1987 Q4 =1)

4.6 Conclusion

In this chapter the problems involved in constructing a data set for estimating the proposed model have been considered. Ideally data relating solely to households would be used in the construction of this data set but generally this is not available in a suitable form. Therefore Personal Sector data is used and although there is some divergence between household and Personal Sector data because of the wider scope of the latter, the construction of the model was shown to mitigate this problem. Another issue addressed was the scope of the model in terms of the assets to be explained. Those assets which are to be explained were aggregated on the basis of two criteria, namely, associated adjustment costs and the scope provided for policy simulations with the model. The two major assets held by households which are not to be explained in the model, equities and wealth held with life assurance and pension funds, are excluded on the grounds that transactions in these assets are not easily explained in an allocation type model.

With regard to rates of return on the various asset categories, two innovatory approaches to the modelling exercise are worth highlighting. Firstly an attempt was made to capture rationing which existed over some of the period of study in the two credit markets modelled. This allowed a role to be found in the model for interest rates on credit. Secondly, proxy rates of return were found for the two physical assets explained in the model.

A final issue addressed was the relationship between inflation, asset accumulation and income. In particular the inflation adjustment of income adopted in recent consumption studies in the Hendry and Ungern-Sternberg tradition (discussed in chapter 3) was related to allocation models such as the one proposed in this study.

Having now established the variables in the model, in the next chapter attention is turned to an examination of the plots of these variables in order to identify trends which will aid specification and understanding of the model.

Notes

1. To see this in nominal terms then we multiply [4.11] through by P ie. :

$$Y - C = A - P * A_{-1}/P_{-1} + (P - P_{-1}) * A_{-1}/P_{-1}$$

$$Y - C = A - P * A_{-1}/P_{-1} + P * A_{-1}/P_{-1} - A_{-1}$$

$$Y - C = A - A_{-1}$$

Thus saving is equal to the change in the net asset stock (ignoring price changes).

Appendix 4A
The generation of expectational variables

The four expectational variables used in the model, namely expected inflation, the expected return on public sector debt and expected capital gains on dwellings and consumer durables were generated using the McCallum (1976) technique.

To illustrate the McCallum technique, suppose that $E_t x_{t+1}$ represents the expected value at time t of the value of x at time t+1. Now the use of ex-post values of x_{t+1} cannot be used as a proxy for $E_t x_{t+1}$ as clearly agents in the personal sector do not possess perfect foresight. The McCallum technique involves the construction of a regression equation to explain the observations x_{t+1} as follows :

$$x_{t+1} = a_i Q_{it} + v_t \qquad [4.A.1]$$

If equation [4.A.1] is correctly specified then it represents all the information available to the personal sector at time t, regarding the formation of the value of x at time t+1 (ie. Q_{it} represents the information set available to the personal sector for forming expectations about the value of x in period t+1). Assuming rational behaviour by agents of the personal sector then it follows that the expected value of x_{t+1} will be determined by the expected value of equation [4.A.1]. Thus using the expectations operator, E :

$$_tE x_{t+1} = E_t(a_iQ_{it}) + E_t(v_t) \qquad [4.A.2]$$

$$= a_iQ_{it}$$

Thus the predictions of equation [4.A.1] can be substituted for $_tE x_{t+1}$ with no measurement error.

(1) Expected capital gains on public sector debt

As outlined in chapter 4, the capital gain element of the return on public sector debt is a four quarter moving average of capital gains :

$$E_tCG_{t+1} = 1/4 \ E_t \ (CG_{t+1} + CG_t + CG_{t-1} + CG_{t-2}) \qquad [4.A.3]$$

This requires a forecast of capital gains accruing in time t+1. Capital gains are proxied by $(P_t - P_{t-1})/P_{t-1}$ where P is the FT Government Securities Index for all stocks. Actual capital gains is instrumented using variables dated t and earlier. These variables were lagged values of the dependent variable and capital gains on equities, housing and life assurance and pension fund equity. Summary statistics for the regression are reported below :

Dependent variable	:	CG_{t+1}
Sample period	:	1971(1) to 1987(4)
R^2	:	0.88

The residuals from this regression were further regressed on up to eight lags of itself and the information set to check for white noise properties. A χ^2 test supports the null hypothesis that the residuals are information free. The results of this analysis are shown in the following table :

lag(L)	R^2	nR^2	χ^2_L (0.05)
1	0.022	1.232	3.84
2	0.023	1.288	5.99
3	0.037	2.072	7.82
4	0.096	5.378	9.49
5	0.118	6.608	11.07
6	0.170	9.520	12.59
7	0.173	9.688	14.07
8	0.194	10.860	15.51

(2) Expected inflation

As described in chapter four the expected inflation variable used in this research is partly forward looking involving the use of the price level four quarters ahead. Thus the four quarter ahead expected price level is generated using the McCallum technique. The problem with such an approach is that the residuals from this process (which can only exploit the one quarter lagged information set) could exhibit up to fourth order serial correlation. Thus the test for white noise of these residuals needs to allow for this problem.

The dependent variable, the price level one year ahead P_{t+4} , was regressed on lagged values of itself, the rate of interest on bank time deposits and the unemployment rate. The summary statistics of this regression are outlined below :

Dependent variable : P_{t+4}
Sample period : 1973(1) to 1987(4)
R^2 : 0.998

The residuals from this regression were then regressed on their own lags of up to four quarters to allow for problem outlined earlier. The residuals from this equation were then regressed on the information set used to generate the expected series and own lags of up to eight quarters. The following table shows the resulting χ^2 statistics which generally support the null hypothesis that the residuals are information free.

Lag(L)	R^2	nR^2	$\chi^2_L(0.05)$
1	0.123	4.92	3.84
2	0.124	4.96	5.99
3	0.137	5.47	7.82
4	0.142	5.69	9.49
5	0.192	7.65	11.07
6	0.235	9.41	12.59
7	0.244	9.76	14.07
8	0.265	10.62	15.51

(3) Expected capital gains on dwellings and consumer durables

The final two variables requiring the generation of expected series are both capital gain variables. The procedure for their generation is therefore the same as for capital gains on public sector debt, as described above. The instrument set for estimating expected capital gains on dwellings includes lagged capital gains on dwellings, capital gains on equities and capital gains on Life Assurance and Pension Fund wealth. The instrument set for expected capital gains on consumer durables includes lagged prices of consumer durables and housing. The results are shown below:

Dependent variable   : $CGDWE_{t+1}$
Estimation period   : 1973(4) to 1987(4)
R^2 : 0.85

Dependent variable   : $CGCD_{t+1}$
Estimation period   : 1972(4) to 1987(4)
R^2 : 0.99

Lag(L)	CGCD nR^2	CGCDWE nR^2	$\chi^2_L (0.05)$
1	1.15	3.90	3.84
2	2.64	5.32	5.99
3	2.65	6.81	7.82
4	4.18	11.18	9.49
5	4.39	12.14	11.07
6	4.73	13.17	12.59
7	4.84	14.14	14.07
8	4.86	15.52	15.51

The χ^2 statistics shown in the above table comfortably support the hypothesis that the residuals for expected series for capital gain on consumer durables are information free. The support for the same hypothesis for the expected capital gain on dwellings residuals is less clear cut but the serial correlation revealed is not seen as serious.

5 Discussion of trends in the data

5.1 Introduction

In the last chapter we considered various issues concerned with the construction of the variables in the proposed model. In this chapter we begin by defining the period over which the model is estimated (section 5.2) and then examine trends in the time series observations of the assets/liabilities to be explained in the model, beginning with financial assets (section 5.3), followed by physical assets (section 5.4) and ending with financial liabilities (section 5.5). The main objective of this chapter is to identify any particular features in the data which will aid the specification of the model to be discussed in chapter 6.

5.2 Defining the estimation period

The observations of the variables in the model are quarterly and are not adjusted for seasonal fluctuations. The earliest date for a consistent set of published quarterly data on personal sector financial stock variables is 1966 Q4. However there is no reliable data showing the split between bank time deposits, sight deposits and notes and coin for the personal sector prior to 1975 Q4. Weale (1986) provides data for these three series for the period 1967 Q1 to 1975 Q3 calculated using a constrained estimation technique and based on trends in private sector data, but it is not possible to know how reliable these calculated series are. There is also the problem that the CSO published data on financial and physical asset stocks for the personal sector have been subject to numerous revisions for the period after 1975 but not before. Thus there is more doubt about the reliability of pre-1975 Q4 financial stock data. Therefore allowing for one period lags the estimation period in this study is taken as 1976 Q1 until 1987 Q4. The end point for the estimation period takes into account the greater unreliability of new published data.

The actual data used in this study is listed in appendix 5.A.

5.3 Financial Assets

5.3.1 Liquid assets

Plots of the real stock of the four liquid assets categories modelled in this study are shown in figures 5.1 to 5.4. Building Society deposits and National Savings both show strong growth in real terms over the 1980's whilst bank time deposits show a real decline. Transaction stocks also show real growth in the 1980's although this is not as strong.

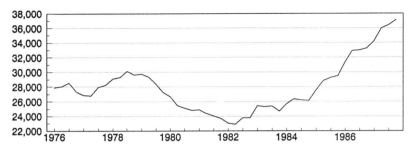

Figure 5.1 : Real Transaction Stocks (1976-87) [£m]

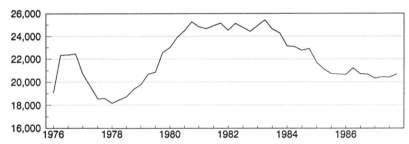

Figure 5.2: Real Stock of Bank Time Deposits (1976-87) [£m]

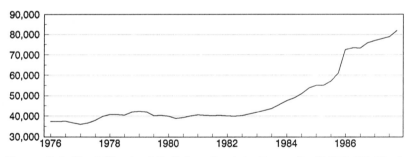

Figure 5.3: Real Stock of Building Society Deposits (1976-87) [£m]

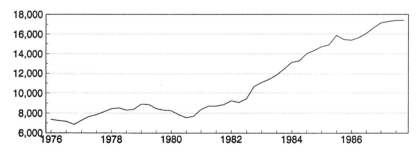

Figure 5.4: Real Stock of National Savings (1976-87) [£m]

The shares of the three components of total interest earning liquid assets can be seen more clearly in figure 5.5. It is clear from this that building society deposits has been the strongest of the interest earning liquid assets over the period. The building societies increased their share of this market over the latter part of the 1970's following the introduction and promotion of term shares by most societies. Over the period 1979 to 1982 the building societies lost some of this share as a result of increased competition from banks and the national savings industry. From 1982 the share of building society deposits has increased even more rapidly as the building societies continued to innovate with the introduction of premium accounts (where higher rates of interest than on ordinary shares are paid in exchange for a short notice period or a minimum sum).

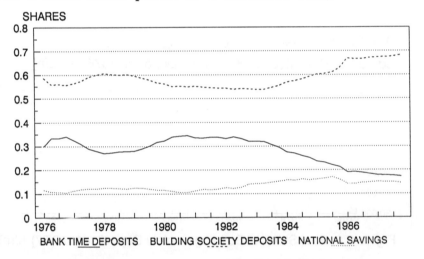

SHARES

BANK TIME DEPOSITS   BUILDING SOCIETY DEPOSITS   NATIONAL SAVINGS

Figure 5.5: Shares in Total Interest Earning Liquid Assets

The greater competitiveness of bank time deposits and the resulting increase in share over the period 1979 to 1982 is partly explained by reference to figure 5.6 which shows real interest rates on the three interest earning liquid assets. The rate of interest on bank time deposits is closer to the rates on the other two categories over this period. Over the period 1983 to 1987 however the interest rate on bank time deposits has become as uncompetitive as the period before 1979 and this has lead to a dramatic decline in share.

The National Savings (NS) instruments made up a relatively small but stable part of interest earning liquid assets up until the beginning of 1981. At this time the rates of interest on the components of this asset were made more competitive (see figure 5.6) and greater promotion of NS products occurred as the Government sought to increase funding through the medium of national savings. As a result, NS instruments (particularly NS certificates) increased their share of interest earning liquid assets until 1984 and after this time the share appears to have stabilised.

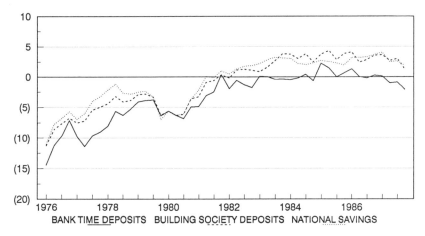

BANK TIME DEPOSITS   BUILDING SOCIETY DEPOSITS   NATIONAL SAVINGS

Figure 5.6: Real Rates of Interest on Liquid Assets (%)

Turning now to transaction stocks (defined as notes and coin plus bank sight deposits plus National Savings ordinary deposits) this also formed a declining share of total liquid assets until around the end of 1982. This can be seen clearly in figure 5.7. This decline is due to many factors including the increasing financial sophistication of households and their search for the best return for their funds held in liquid form, the heavy marketing of building society products since the 1970's, the decline in cash holdings as a result of the increased use of credit for transaction purposes. Also it would be expected that during times of high inflation, such as over the period 1973-1982 (see figure 5.8) that households would prefer to hold liquid funds in interest earning form, as this compensates to some extent for the inflation erosion of the stock.

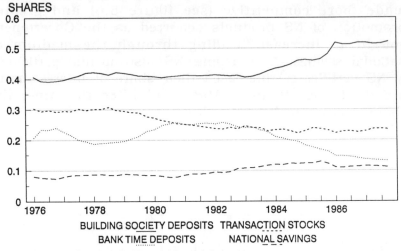

Figure 5.7: Shares in Total Liquid Assets

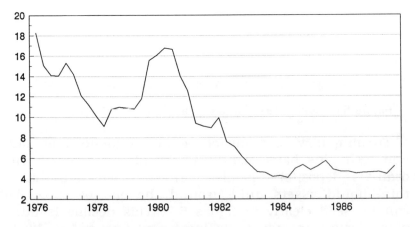

Figure 5.8: Expected Inflation (%)

The stability of the share (relative to the early part of the period) from the end of 1984 is probably accounted for by the reduction in inflationary expectations making it less costly (in terms of the relative erosion of the asset stock) to hold non-interest earning balances. The introduction of interest earning sight deposits from the end of 1983, as banks attempted to attract Personal Sector customers in order to sell other financial products, is also likely to have been a factor in explaining the stability of the share.

The discussion in this section would suggest firstly that real interest rates appear to play an important role in determining allocation decisions - thus supporting the use of an allocation model - and secondly that there are other factors such as financial innovation which also appear to play a role but which are more difficult to model. It was mentioned in chapter four though that the innovation of new financial products such as interest bearing sight deposits will be accounted for in the model by a trend variable beginning in 1983 Q4.

5.3.2 Illiquid assets

The other financial asset explained in the model - public sector debt - consisting of government securities ended the period with approximately the same share of total financial assets (explained in the model) as it began. This can be seen in figure 5.9. Over the period though the share has fluctuated reflecting capital gains/losses on the asset.

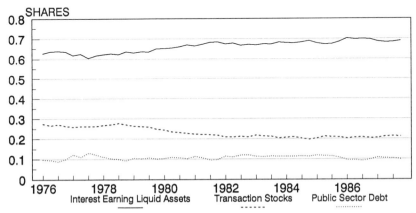

Figure 5.9: Shares in Total Financial Assets (explained in the model)

Of the two financial assets not explained in the model (but included as explanatory variables - see chapter 4), namely the stock of Life Assurance and Pension Funds (LAPF) and company shares, EQUITY, it is clear from figure 5.10 that over the first half of the estimation period there has been a shift in wealth holdings from EQUITY to LAPF. This implies a shift from direct to indirect holdings of equities and there are many reasons for this which were briefly mentioned in chapter 4. The share of EQUITY in total financial assets has stabilised though in the 1980's and increased from 1986. This is partly due to an increased acquisition of equities by households following the Government's promotion of wider share ownership through the privatisation issues, and partly to the bull market in equities from 1981 to 1987 which saw the accrual of large capital gains. Indeed it is argued that the accrual of large capital gains to illiquid financial assets such as LAPF and EQUITY over the 1980's may have had an effect on consumption - saving behaviour.

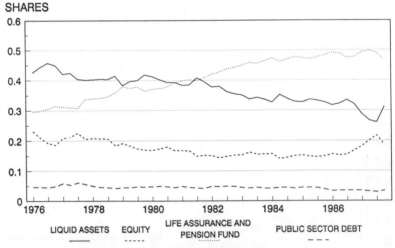

Figure 5.10: Shares in Total Financial Assets

Davis (1988) argues that the magnitude of capital gains on EQUITY, LAPF and housing may partly explain the decline in the level of saving over the 1980's. This follows from the hypothesis that households have a target level of wealth and that when wealth accrues in the form of capital gain (and when developments in the credit markets make it easier to realise this gain - discussed in chapter 4 and below) then there is less need to accrue wealth through financial acquisition. This provides a reason for the inclusion of EQUITY and LAPF as explanatory variables in the model.

5.4 Physical assets

The two physical assets explained in the model are consumer durables and housing and the shares of these in total physical assets over the estimation period are shown in figure 5.11.

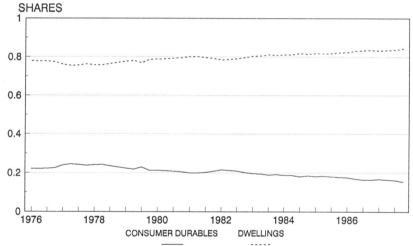

Figure 5.11: Shares in Total Physical Assets

The share of consumer durable stocks can be seen to have fallen relative to dwellings over the period. This reflects the increasing trend to owner occupation and hence increased investment in housing and house price price changes leading to capital gains. Clearly it is capital gains which have dominated the increasing value of the housing stock since the late 1970's. As stated earlier capital gains are likely to have had an effect on other financial decisions of households and it could in fact be argued that capital gains on housing are likely to have a stronger effect on other decisions, because of the wider ownership of the asset across households (compared to EQUITY) and the ease of realising the gain, particularly since 1980 (compared to LAPF).

One effect of the large capital gain on other household decisions is a direct one on consumption and other asset acquisition as the gain is realised. Another less direct effect stems from the argument that these capital gains make households feel more wealthy and thus in the long term leads to a reduction in acquisition of other types of assets. (ie. a reduction in the level of saving as experienced over the 1980's).

5.5 Liabilities

The real stock of the two liabilities explained in the model - consumer credit and loans for house purchase - are shown in figures 5.12 and 5.13. Both these liabilities have grown in real terms over the period of study, but the rate of growth was significantly faster after 1980. There are a number of reasons for this with the main one being the relaxation of controls on lending. For consumer lending this involved the removal of the "Corset" on banks and the abolition of the minimum deposit on hire purchase transactions. The growth in mortgage lending was also influenced by the removal of the "Corset" on bank lending which prompted the entry of banks into the mortgage market resulting in greater competition which also helped to bring about the break up of the Building Societies cartel arrangement on interest rate setting. These institutional changes in the personal sector credit markets are discussed in greater detail in chapter four. The effect of this greater availability of credit for households was that it allowed them to restructure their balance sheet so that, for example, transaction balances declined (due to increased use of credit for transaction purposes) and other assets increased (especially physical assets as it became easier to finance their acquisition through credit). Another reason advanced to explain the growth in personal sector borrowing in the 1980's is the increased level of owner occupation of housing over the 1980's - requiring loans to finance the purchase of housing - especially as a result of the transfer of over one million homes from council to private ownership (from 1979 to 1987). Furthermore loans for house purchase is one of the means by which households have realised capital gain built up in housing.

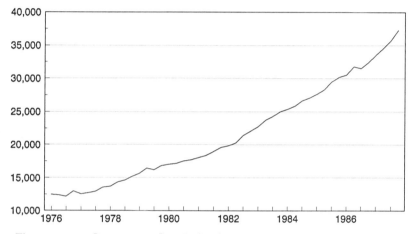

Figure 5.12: Consumer Credit (£m)

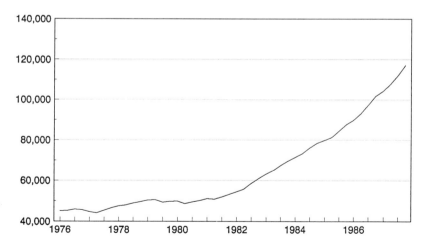

Figure 5.13: Loans For House Purchase (£m)

The increased availability and use of credit over the 1980's provides a further explanation for the fall in the level of saving if we note that saving equals purchases of assets less borrowing) over this period (Davis, (1987)).

5.6 Conclusion

The discussion of trends in the variables in this chapter appears to provide evidence for the view that relative interest rates play a significant role in explaining the allocation of funds to financial assets. This supports the use of a portfolio type model to model financial behaviour. The discussion has also reinforced the central theme of this research that households expenditure and financial decisions are, and have become increasingly, interrelated and should therefore be modelled as such. Another feature highlighted by this discussion of trends in the data is a significant change in financial markets after 1980. The 1980's has seen greater competition between financial institutions following deregulation and the ending of restrictions on lending. The restructuring of the Personal Sector balance sheet that took place as a consequence should be captured to some extent by the introduction of a dummy variable beginning in 1980 quarter three which is designed to pick up this environment change (discussed in chapter four, section four).

In the next chapter we move on to examine the specification of the model and the issues involved in estimating the model.

Appendix 5A
The data

This appendix contains data on all the variables used to construct the model. The data are seasonally unadjusted. The dependent variables are deflated by the implicit consumer price deflator (base = 1980) and the variable name is therefore given a prefix D. All variables are defined in chapter 4.

	DCON	DTRS	DBTD	DBSD
1976:1	26968.17383	27893.87305	19098.85156	37367.16797
1976:2	27907.18945	28061.23438	22348.18945	37441.21094
1976:3	28666.48438	28543.78906	22366.50000	37498.89453
1976:4	30274.23633	27353.92188	22491.45703	36743.34375
1977:1	26954.93750	26885.81055	20710.98438	36093.19531
1977:2	27710.74805	26794.83203	19657.60938	36712.92578
1977:3	28506.96094	27964.08008	18571.66211	37964.75391
1977:4	30715.18555	28306.50781	18596.04883	39927.63672
1978:1	28405.25781	29110.42188	18165.89648	40771.15234
1978:2	29102.55664	29316.68359	18460.43750	40805.94531
1978:3	30065.25781	30145.50586	18726.65430	40502.71875
1978:4	31971.84961	29667.84961	19378.28125	41991.41797
1979:1	29220.28320	29768.35156	19811.12891	42271.89063
1979:2	30692.89453	29394.38672	20721.46875	42080.65234
1979:3	30913.71484	28403.51563	20872.91797	40242.66797
1979:4	32905.29688	27304.69922	22566.49414	40378.26563
1980:1	30173.23047	26687.72266	22993.04102	39975.55469
1980:2	30229.65430	25479.25000	23912.50000	38914.98828
1980:3	31237.63477	25113.93555	24481.05859	39415.97656
1980:4	32625.26172	24814.26563	25277.55664	40186.94141
1981:1	29837.46680	24920.47070	24823.94727	40749.13281
1981:2	30335.53711	24422.79102	24673.80859	40378.00391
1981:3	31094.13477	24086.57422	24944.50000	40311.16016
1981:4	32814.73828	23727.47461	25132.44727	40405.19531
1982:1	29641.72461	23097.09961	24505.21289	40132.92969
1982:2	30320.21289	22947.68945	25116.27148	39951.74219
1982:3	31374.16797	23780.55078	24768.91016	40243.50781
1982:4	33395.00391	23785.90234	24413.78125	41142.83984
1983:1	30469.28320	25440.40430	24937.59375	41838.13672
1983:2	31351.87500	25306.83008	25452.12891	42818.81250
1983:3	32508.23242	25377.38086	24627.00586	43884.53906
1983:4	34359.79688	24731.71484	24281.82617	45721.96484
1984:1	31262.01563	25708.93945	23138.57227	47718.08594
1984:2	32206.60547	26398.78516	23082.02539	49065.38672
1984:3	32778.51172	26227.48242	22777.15039	50998.77344
1984:4	35051.51953	26136.37695	22901.60938	53942.21875
1985:1	32290.19531	27576.03906	21722.09570	55203.98438
1985:2	32921.31641	28847.54297	21146.82422	55174.42188
1985:3	34051.90234	29262.92969	20744.58789	57174.00391
1985:4	36644.64453	29523.78711	20684.59766	61053.32422
1986:1	33804.60547	31409.74219	20644.74414	72638.76563
1986:2	34997.18359	32922.60156	21236.32422	73533.08594
1986:3	35941.07813	32998.59375	20736.48633	73445.47656
1986:4	38420.27734	33263.75000	20716.60156	76041.90625
1987:1	35148.34766	34239.50781	20334.06250	77083.21875
1987:2	36434.96875	35985.66406	20466.91211	78046.30469
1987:3	38062.91797	36450.96484	20437.75586	78969.18750
1987:4	40969.83594	37127.31641	20693.03516	82024.57813

All figures in £million

	DNATSAV	DPSD	DDWE	DCD
1976:1	7374.46143	9907.59375	226353.73437	64229.93359
1976:2	7250.14307	10011.22559	224916.84375	63881.10156
1976:3	7170.30225	9287.20117	226963.04688	64693.54297
1976:4	6859.74512	10364.43652	224196.31250	65347.86719
1977:1	7277.84814	12734.35547	218263.31250	68660.63281
1977:2	7644.14551	11330.84766	211989.67188	69010.94531
1977:3	7833.41016	13962.85449	219837.15625	70558.92969
1977:4	8136.47266	13143.20898	224047.59375	70114.59375
1978:1	8428.84375	11858.06348	232302.40625	73789.46094
1978:2	8530.29102	10974.01660	235875.78125	75225.23438
1978:3	8291.82227	10743.98145	248990.15625	76400.45313
1978:4	8400.85547	10097.99707	262527.37500	78040.16406
1979:1	8897.62109	11736.24219	275804.84375	79309.13281
1979:2	8861.19434	11458.21094	281677.87500	78791.34375
1979:3	8432.04590	11593.92090	279911.65625	83431.78906
1979:4	8301.21875	11004.04395	297988.09375	80609.21094
1980:1	8260.20605	11241.99121	298118.75000	80185.84375
1980:2	7837.76318	11768.68164	290857.84375	77548.91406
1980:3	7551.35205	11537.98730	293979.75000	77025.50781
1980:4	7704.96484	11160.06738	292878.46875	75623.98438
1981:1	8343.99512	12564.72266	296727.25000	73834.92188
1981:2	8690.01172	11562.86035	287719.96875	71548.96094
1981:3	8688.46484	10371.11816	280609.90625	71472.39844
1981:4	8860.68359	10567.76367	274579.90625	72167.31250
1982:1	9240.01465	12594.14551	265724.06250	72798.59375
1982:2	9058.83496	12143.88965	265893.90625	71925.39844
1982:3	9436.77734	13429.88281	272547.06250	72002.87500
1982:4	10633.19922	13586.46680	279519.50000	71076.20313
1983:1	11072.85059	13168.54688	284451.81250	69523.07813
1983:2	11400.89355	13236.94043	293779.90625	71030.37500
1983:3	11852.20801	13734.29199	306506.75000	71384.33594
1983:4	12477.37793	13545.38867	312181.84375	74005.39063
1984:1	13145.29199	13988.78711	314870.75000	73022.01563
1984:2	13278.80078	14142.73145	319105.15625	73952.52344
1984:3	14029.79004	14861.16895	336381.40625	74281.62500
1984:4	14362.60156	14991.90625	333748.21875	75874.10156
1985:1	14723.38477	16130.52148	335972.18750	74675.14844
1985:2	14926.71973	15717.91309	338756.31250	76064.75781
1985:3	15874.58887	16044.26367	345742.18750	76522.35938
1985:4	15453.28223	15248.37500	362575.21875	78370.29688
1986:1	15420.88477	14799.23926	367664.25000	78537.74219
1986:2	15659.20898	15065.51367	391687.28125	79638.42188
1986:3	16104.16211	14518.98438	401595.84375	79513.00781
1986:4	16672.50195	15787.97852	409958.96875	80613.38281
1987:1	17171.11719	18039.38867	419008.50000	84290.79688
1987:2	17292.04883	17809.23242	431436.87500	84674.89844
1987:3	17413.09766	17577.11133	447435.65625	86658.14063
1987:4	17402.09375	17241.85547	471584.65625	86535.26563

All figures in £million

	DCONCR	DLHP	EQUITY	LAPF
1976:1	-12503.01660	-45080.76172	49705.80859	63587.85938
1976:2	-12397.24219	-45225.48828	44837.02734	64045.71875
1976:3	-12179.53418	-45920.68750	40116.39063	63801.45703
1976:4	-12976.02246	-45631.87500	38679.19531	65368.40625
1977:1	-12585.58301	-44732.54297	44974.48438	67248.33594
1977:2	-12724.88086	-44243.30078	45478.92188	66245.42188
1977:3	-12942.46484	-45408.76563	51532.52734	70347.20313
1977:4	-13551.43555	-46619.18359	48626.64844	79611.17969
1978:1	-13696.18066	-47592.33203	49954.83594	81418.10156
1978:2	-14359.90234	-48042.10547	49882.25781	81970.55469
1978:3	-14619.55078	-49051.07031	49950.89844	83865.41406
1978:4	-15186.85352	-49721.12891	44287.70313	86142.83594
1979:1	-15662.18262	-50525.68750	50437.49219	99849.40625
1979:2	-16455.46289	-50690.40625	46668.55469	95353.50000
1979:3	-16205.60352	-49444.46094	42614.35547	92812.67188
1979:4	-16833.73047	-49770.96875	40170.10156	85908.85938
1980:1	-17030.53906	-49901.67578	40155.91406	88044.83594
1980:2	-17152.00391	-48654.51563	41705.44531	89521.42188
1980:3	-17533.14844	-49532.19922	44418.16016	92969.14844
1980:4	-17694.86328	-50204.54297	42100.28516	97668.50000
1981:1	-18044.91992	-51127.58594	43313.99219	102613.14844
1981:2	-18373.37109	-50921.60938	42779.19141	102506.04688
1981:3	-18942.51367	-52033.81641	36199.75391	95883.26563
1981:4	-19577.78320	-53243.91797	38044.98047	101624.92969
1982:1	-19844.50586	-54514.49219	38944.67578	107748.42188
1982:2	-20316.39258	-55810.40625	37005.17578	109202.94531
1982:3	-21425.80664	-58569.86328	40460.44531	118465.64063
1982:4	-22093.98438	-61028.86328	42974.55078	124779.33594
1983:1	-22762.17578	-63169.24219	45176.25391	132007.51563
1983:2	-23727.96875	-65061.94141	50330.05469	142168.90625
1983:3	-24321.78320	-67562.81250	47879.35547	140568.14063
1983:4	-25035.44727	-69655.90625	49787.71484	147835.34375
1984:1	-25392.15820	-71493.98438	52791.85156	158690.82813
1984:2	-25877.48633	-73340.74219	44694.26563	146425.60938
1984:3	-26655.94531	-76158.38281	48930.17969	157726.92188
1984:4	-27078.16211	-78507.50781	53832.26953	169444.12500
1985:1	-27613.01367	-79790.83594	55650.51563	172839.60938
1985:2	-28295.45117	-81405.10156	52917.94922	167891.26563
1985:3	-29452.68750	-84551.12500	54375.41797	176202.26563
1985:4	-30201.76758	-87716.66406	58104.86328	186720.39063
1986:1	-30544.19531	-89800.25781	68869.49219	217421.70313
1986:2	-31818.30078	-92950.12500	67876.22656	216914.45313
1986:3	-31541.92773	-97221.15625	66575.48438	202866.34375
1986:4	-32431.41406	-101752.53125	76738.82031	217460.57813
1987:1	-33512.56641	-104453.10156	94071.13281	254152.56250
1987:2	-34569.22656	-107777.92188	114600.86719	282209.87500
1987:3	-35685.34766	-112117.42969	127278.53125	288190.93750
1987:4	-37292.02344	-117168.39063	94027.09375	235279.04688

All figures in £million

	PE	RBTD	RBSD	RNATSAV
1976:1	-18.25595	-14.43595	-11.25595	-10.98325
1976:2	-15.08080	-11.23080	-8.58080	-7.76943
1976:3	-14.09090	-9.59090	-7.59090	-6.75305
1976:4	-14.08030	-7.10030	-6.72030	-5.67521
1977:1	-15.33310	-9.71310	-7.53310	-6.93239
1977:2	-14.21563	-11.39563	-7.21563	-6.02364
1977:3	-12.11365	-9.62365	-5.41365	-3.98029
1977:4	-11.21617	-9.02617	-4.98617	-3.27461
1978:1	-10.08146	-8.06146	-4.42146	-2.18005
1978:2	-9.10883	-5.63883	-3.20883	-1.19332
1978:3	-10.81493	-6.29493	-4.11493	-2.68340
1978:4	-11.00461	-5.26462	-3.87461	-2.82825
1979:1	-10.90708	-4.08708	-2.90708	-2.52014
1979:2	-10.80193	-3.85193	-2.80193	-2.35157
1979:3	-11.82000	-3.77000	-3.32000	-3.30553
1979:4	-15.57820	-6.37820	-6.24820	-6.98032
1980:1	-16.08944	-5.58944	-5.58944	-5.64370
1980:2	-16.79992	-6.29992	-6.29992	-6.38152
1980:3	-16.66991	-6.82991	-6.16991	-6.01279
1980:4	-14.07566	-4.90566	-3.57566	-3.69751
1981:1	-12.52455	-4.86455	-3.27455	-2.18127
1981:2	-9.39409	-3.09409	-0.89409	0.06926
1981:3	-9.11240	-2.51240	-0.61240	-0.10118
1981:4	-8.94659	0.36341	0.38341	1.02101
1982:1	-9.92442	-1.93442	-0.17442	0.47592
1982:2	-7.58243	-0.58243	1.16757	1.31700
1982:3	-7.12173	-1.32173	1.28827	1.74437
1982:4	-6.14159	-1.77159	1.10841	1.89406
1983:1	-5.36314	0.08686	0.88686	2.20309
1983:2	-4.63997	0.05003	1.61003	2.85575
1983:3	-4.59295	-0.39295	2.65705	3.27077
1983:4	-4.19783	-0.34784	3.84216	3.09583
1984:1	-4.26804	-0.43804	3.77196	3.05776
1984:2	-4.08335	-0.16335	3.00665	2.19650
1984:3	-4.99261	0.39739	3.78739	2.01014
1984:4	-5.33226	-0.61226	2.48774	2.34598
1985:1	-4.85153	2.25847	3.75847	2.69725
1985:2	-5.22254	1.48746	4.35746	2.54329
1985:3	-5.71368	0.01632	2.84632	2.28116
1985:4	-4.86360	0.63640	3.84640	1.91044
1986:1	-4.69002	1.31998	4.11998	3.21572
1986:2	-4.68412	0.07588	2.44588	3.19963
1986:3	-4.47874	-0.15874	2.82126	3.31840
1986:4	-4.56522	0.26478	3.57479	3.69720
1987:1	-4.58653	0.15347	3.65347	4.06595
1987:2	-4.64548	-0.97548	2.72452	2.52585
1987:3	-4.43614	-0.86614	2.99386	2.63602
1987:4	-5.20794	-2.09794	1.30206	1.86632

	RPSD	RCONCR	RLHP	LVR
1976:1	-7.21185	3.63405	-11.10595	0.78700
1976:2	-2.02712	6.86921	-8.25080	0.81100
1976:3	-1.33682	8.72910	-7.26090	0.79500
1976:4	0.21503	11.69970	-6.12030	0.78700
1977:1	-5.27855	8.99690	-7.37310	0.78200
1977:2	-3.97164	6.61437	-6.95563	0.77300
1977:3	-0.81478	7.91635	-5.40365	0.78600
1977:4	2.62393	7.33383	-4.94617	0.79300
1978:1	2.20734	8.45854	-4.47146	0.81200
1978:2	0.12691	11.32117	-3.13883	0.81600
1978:3	-4.15138	11.18507	-4.28493	0.79300
1978:4	-3.97349	12.39538	-3.57462	0.77700
1979:1	-3.98595	13.96292	-3.03708	0.77200
1979:2	-2.36662	13.62807	-2.57193	0.77200
1979:3	-4.06869	14.18000	-3.07000	0.75100
1979:4	-6.98722	11.83180	-5.65820	0.73300
1980:1	-8.00867	12.91056	-5.58944	0.73000
1980:2	-8.65797	12.20008	-6.29992	0.72400
1980:3	-10.64067	11.38008	-6.16991	0.72100
1980:4	-3.86688	13.14434	-3.80566	0.77700
1981:1	-1.77095	13.03545	-3.19455	0.78300
1981:2	2.47344	14.60591	-0.29409	0.78600
1981:3	0.56814	15.22760	-0.01240	0.79000
1981:4	-1.02112	18.21341	1.55341	0.80200
1982:1	-0.27436	15.90558	0.22558	0.83200
1982:2	4.05124	17.28757	1.86757	0.84400
1982:3	4.82105	16.22827	1.62827	0.84400
1982:4	7.48825	15.53841	1.32841	0.84400
1983:1	7.37277	17.45686	1.63686	0.84400
1983:2	5.63655	17.36003	2.65003	0.84400
1983:3	5.25151	16.90705	3.28705	0.84400
1983:4	2.51986	16.80217	3.68217	0.84400
1984:1	4.76501	16.65196	3.75196	0.84400
1984:2	5.67761	16.74665	3.29665	0.84400
1984:3	3.32887	17.83739	3.53739	0.84400
1984:4	1.41167	16.66774	3.22774	0.84400
1985:1	2.35237	20.25847	4.16847	0.84400
1985:2	1.95329	19.45746	4.74746	0.84400
1985:3	2.43138	17.95632	3.98632	0.84400
1985:4	3.24311	18.63640	4.26640	0.84400
1986:1	4.28828	19.47998	4.40998	0.84400
1986:2	3.46118	17.74588	3.65588	0.84400
1986:3	3.46520	17.52126	3.36126	0.84400
1986:4	3.48359	18.10479	3.85478	0.84400
1987:1	2.44697	18.24347	4.14347	0.84400
1987:2	2.25045	16.77452	3.86452	0.84400
1987:3	4.31098	17.23386	3.77386	0.84400
1987:4	3.62168	16.02206	2.77206	0.84400

	DNW	DY	T	TR
1976:1	334641.84375	20787.17383	0.00000	0.00000
1976:2	336287.21875	31387.12109	0.00000	0.00000
1976:3	338423.06250	29231.79492	0.00000	0.00000
1976:4	334749.18750	28732.32422	0.00000	0.00000
1977:1	333308.00000	25255.18750	0.00000	0.00000
1977:2	326172.78125	26442.16211	0.00000	0.00000
1977:3	338341.62500	29643.66211	0.00000	0.00000
1977:4	342101.43750	32394.08398	0.00000	0.00000
1978:1	353137.71875	29151.09180	0.00000	0.00000
1978:2	356786.37500	28623.15234	0.00000	0.00000
1978:3	370130.65625	30029.76953	0.00000	0.00000
1978:4	385195.96875	33485.36328	0.00000	0.00000
1979:1	401411.34375	30068.17969	0.00000	0.00000
1979:2	405839.25000	30174.95313	0.00000	0.00000
1979:3	407238.43750	27479.51172	0.00000	0.00000
1979:4	421547.31250	33574.79297	0.00000	0.00000
1980:1	420530.90625	29352.98828	0.00000	0.00000
1980:2	410513.40625	28448.24414	0.00000	0.00000
1980:3	412040.21875	30624.01758	1.00000	0.00000
1980:4	409746.84375	34099.41797	1.00000	0.00000
1981:1	412791.93750	29976.33008	1.00000	0.00000
1981:2	399701.43750	28874.77148	1.00000	0.00000
1981:3	389507.78125	29674.92969	1.00000	0.00000
1981:4	382619.09375	32719.22852	1.00000	0.00000
1982:1	373733.06250	26935.79297	1.00000	0.00000
1982:2	370910.93750	28778.51367	1.00000	0.00000
1982:3	376213.90625	30703.83789	1.00000	0.00000
1982:4	381035.03125	33365.89844	1.00000	0.00000
1983:1	384501.00000	31423.41406	1.00000	0.00000
1983:2	394235.96875	32119.89844	1.00000	0.00000
1983:3	405481.90625	32651.98633	1.00000	0.00000
1983:4	412254.15625	35638.53516	1.00000	1.00000
1984:1	414706.31250	32793.62500	1.00000	2.00000
1984:2	419807.18750	32998.42188	1.00000	3.00000
1984:3	436743.06250	34375.03125	1.00000	4.00000
1984:4	436371.37500	37734.84766	1.00000	5.00000
1985:1	438599.50000	34213.75391	1.00000	6.00000
1985:2	440933.93750	32706.60352	1.00000	7.00000
1985:3	447361.09375	35150.79688	1.00000	8.00000
1985:4	464990.43750	38533.13672	1.00000	9.00000
1986:1	480770.90625	45940.24219	1.00000	10.00000
1986:2	504974.00000	35856.05469	1.00000	11.00000
1986:3	510149.46875	33875.80469	1.00000	12.00000
1986:4	518871.15625	40849.10156	1.00000	13.00000
1987:1	532200.93750	35052.63672	1.00000	14.00000
1987:2	543364.81250	38740.00781	1.00000	15.00000
1987:3	557139.12500	35787.87891	1.00000	16.00000
1987:4	578148.37500	42928.37500	1.00000	17.00000

	ECGDWE	ECGCD	CGPSD
1976:1	-3732.18823	1763.11804	443.30423
1976:2	-5683.14746	2038.27942	-132.92964
1976:3	3993.43701	1937.18433	-1050.04822
1976:4	-2488.53638	1034.08667	-481.18372
1977:1	-4779.57178	1623.75366	1719.30347
1977:2	-1875.34961	1618.54065	-1063.75989
1977:3	4235.18896	2951.10327	2106.98633
1977:4	4108.92627	1212.29688	-780.11121
1978:1	10704.94043	2096.57520	-969.31818
1978:2	2517.23999	2325.46631	-924.81122
1978:3	5037.83008	3497.18115	-318.93195
1978:4	9378.66992	2091.33228	-820.24524
1979:1	12202.25977	1204.16809	1096.07874
1979:2	979.83685	2771.31836	-652.81146
1979:3	3207.82886	2723.37915	-149.49146
1979:4	15329.99902	1631.13745	-1437.39844
1980:1	-4361.93604	3137.77490	-85.09467
1980:2	-5748.30127	154.88893	-378.17432
1980:3	-1872.11365	2524.53198	-192.00623
1980:4	-4925.46045	1065.00916	-931.64349
1981:1	-1611.20483	194.93393	925.93567
1981:2	-13501.08105	1180.69983	-1423.52905
1981:3	-3673.79834	983.41089	-1221.77661
1981:4	-2215.14307	159.96571	-743.70862
1982:1	-11165.54102	924.05615	1917.76050
1982:2	-3408.86694	1177.50867	-526.31421
1982:3	-256.49536	815.84351	586.82037
1982:4	1066.30786	-254.19916	277.20090
1983:1	3729.49561	697.61810	56.92514
1983:2	8002.15430	571.71460	-62.38750
1983:3	7878.25244	-263.03299	-296.40649
1983:4	5189.58203	1046.67456	-416.87643
1984:1	4320.50146	679.72003	444.15524
1984:2	5232.61621	1946.21484	329.47064
1984:3	9409.07129	259.10013	-175.31049
1984:4	5527.72998	-29.66448	-52.36945
1985:1	2380.86328	1293.62573	-81.22864
1985:2	3123.87329	2236.95752	-258.43430
1985:3	5390.03271	-241.08635	-129.44482
1985:4	10810.82910	684.39130	-469.48615
1986:1	6269.88135	-50.85027	-674.68280
1986:2	18537.11523	920.20776	105.01938
1986:3	9306.71484	346.90927	-469.24643
1986:4	8680.08203	96.07895	196.03699
1987:1	5096.64844	2154.88867	2265.21631
1987:2	10261.45313	174.94603	-1751.37769
1987:3	18415.71484	1247.46338	581.34882
1987:4	17717.49609	-507.25385	-1443.57520

	UCGDWE	UCGCD
1976:1	-820.76538	-445.09302
1976:2	2954.52905	-1011.28735
1976:3	-3147.06738	-162.97156
1976:4	-1599.08252	1402.75220
1977:1	-2386.98291	4082.06079
1977:2	-5598.43994	1052.37610
1977:3	2373.41846	-634.55518
1977:4	-1265.24512	-1194.95227
1978:1	-3912.39453	2370.64404
1978:2	-166.79565	376.96143
1978:3	6748.40039	-1584.70959
1978:4	2677.33203	224.70923
1979:1	-355.29590	1220.26721
1979:2	3446.02344	-1598.51990
1979:3	-6448.17529	5499.84863
1979:4	776.34277	-2660.70239
1980:1	2773.31543	-1660.22302
1980:2	-2912.81885	648.31476
1980:3	3496.09570	-1816.07727
1980:4	2212.37891	-1187.81702
1981:1	4085.32275	-688.75714
1981:2	3010.19141	-896.01550
1981:3	-4899.11865	36.83136
1981:4	-5064.33301	1070.04187
1982:1	1114.86328	1028.76196
1982:2	2098.05347	-620.80737
1982:3	5460.14746	-633.01685
1982:4	4405.65576	-644.73297
1983:1	70.49414	-2042.69568
1983:2	-223.07178	678.53491
1983:3	3196.92529	586.44617
1983:4	-1209.75146	883.88342
1984:1	-2980.24146	-1543.58911
1984:2	-2737.85400	-461.38757
1984:3	6007.88965	-161.39410
1984:4	-9852.47559	1351.76477
1985:1	-1385.34399	-1903.34985
1985:2	-2101.83887	-451.40662
1985:3	-250.26807	559.02911
1985:4	4283.91895	431.19806
1986:1	-2355.06152	455.54562
1986:2	3625.74805	156.13147
1986:3	-1512.10547	-431.52924
1986:4	-2436.41113	-242.92218
1987:1	2530.19678	1378.54248
1987:2	123.45117	50.36484
1987:3	-4789.76855	594.59143
1987:4	4276.26172	-992.21783

6   Estimation of the model

6.1 Introduction

The main objectives of this chapter are to set out the specification of the model, to consider alternative approaches to estimation and to discuss the estimation results.

To begin though, in section 6.2, the main findings of the theoretical and empirical surveys of earlier chapters, relevant to the specification of the model, are summarised. An objective of this study is to find a parsimonious system of equations describing consumption expenditure and asset accumulation by the personal sector. In sections 6.3 and 6.4 two approaches to achieving such a system of equations will be discussed. These can be labelled the conventional approach and the cointegration approach. It is argued that the cointegration approach has advantages over the conventional approach when it comes to modelling heavily parametised systems of equations. In sections 6.5 and 6.6 some practical issues concerned with the specification and testing of the model are outlined. This is followed in the final sections with a discussion of the results from applying the cointegration approach to estimating the model.

6.2 Summary of the theoretical and empirical issues

The main lesson from the survey of the theoretical background to modelling household decisions presented in chapter two is that the commonly adopted assumption of separability of preferences is overly restrictive. In this study separability of preferences is not assumed and therefore consumption and asset demands are modelled in a simultaneous system of equations. The long run or desired asset stock and consumption expenditure demands are therefore specified as follows:

LONG RUN : $a^*_t = Kx_t$ [6.1]

where a^*_t = vector of long run desired real asset stocks and real consumption.

ie. $(C/P, A_1/P, A_2/P, ... A_n/P)$

x_t = vector of variables determining a^*_t

K = matrix of long run parameters

The long run or desired demands are specified in levels rather than shares as it was noted in chapter three that the denominator in a shares specification in this study (equal to consumption plus net wealth) is difficult to interpret. This rules out consideration of the standard AIDS framework which is specified in shares. A further lesson from the empirical survey of chapter three is that it is useful to test for the restrictions of symmetry and homogeneity in such heavily parametised models. It was also noted that in considering the appropriate form of dynamics for such a model such restrictions are more likely to be accepted by the data when a general form of dynamics was introduced. Therefore short run adjustment towards the long run position is modelled by assuming the generalised version of the quadratic cost function (see chapter 3, section 3.3 for a discussion):

$$TC = (a - a^*)_t' \, C_1 \, (a - a^*)_t + \Delta a_t' \, C_2 \, \Delta a_t$$
$$- \Delta a_t \, C_3 \, \Delta a^*_t \qquad [6.2]$$

where C_i (i=1,2,3) are conformable adjustment matrices.

Minimising TC with respect to a_t results in the following first order condition :

$$(C_1 + C_1') \, (a_t - a^*_t) + (C_2 + C_2') \, \Delta a_t - C_3 \, \Delta a^*_t = 0$$

Letting $D_1 = C_1 + C_1'$, $D_2 = C_2 + C_2'$ and $D = D_1 + D_2$ this equation can be re-arranged to yield the following generalised error feedback model :

$$\Delta a_t = D^{-1}(D_1 + C_3) \, \Delta a^*_t + D^{-1}D_1 \, (a^*_{t-1} - a_{t-1}) \qquad [6.3]$$

Substituting [6.1] into [6.3] , letting $D^{-1}(D_1 + C_3)K = B_2$, $D^{-1}D_1 = B_1$ and $B_1K = B_3$ and adding an error term yields the following short run general model :

SHORT RUN $\quad \Delta a_t = -B_1 \, a_{t-1} + B_2 \, \Delta x_t + B_3 \, x_{t-1} + u_t$ [6.4]

Two approaches to obtaining a parsimonious set of dynamic asset equations integrated with a consumption equation can be identified. The first which can be called the conventional approach is to investigate various simplifications to the general model described by [6.1] and [6.4]. Firstly dynamic simplification can be examined by testing down to the partial adjustment and static models. Secondly appropriate aggregation of asset categories can be tested for. Third, exclusion restrictions on variables in x_t can be examined although this is severely limited by the nature of the specification and the need to satisfy adding up constraints. Finally restrictions derived from utility theory, namely interest rate homogeneity and symmetry can be investigated. The second approach involves the use of cointegration techniques and uses the model described by [6.1] and

[6.3]. The conventional approach will be described first and then compared with the cointegration approach.

6.3 The conventional approach

With this approach the model described by [6.1] and [6.4] would represent the maintained model. Various simplifications can then be tested against the alternative of the maintained model. The discussion that follows draws on Hood (1987).

Nested within the general model of [6.1] and [6.4] are a number of important models (see Anderson and Blundell, 1982). These include firstly the multivariate partial adjustment model (obtained by dropping the last term from the cost function defined by [6.2]).

$$\Delta a_t = E_1 \, x_t + E_2 \, a_{t-1} \qquad \qquad [6.5]$$

The second nested model is the static model simply described by [6.1] - implying instantaneous adjustment to changes in the long run determining variables. These two nested models can therefore be easily tested against the more general model.

Of the two previous attempts to model Personal Sector integrated financial decision making Backus & Purvis (1980) and Owen (1986), described in chapter 3, the multivariate partial adjustment framework is used for the dynamic specification (although Owen (1986), pg 196) mentions that he estimated a version of the general specification of [6.4], but found it was rejected by the data for 6 out of 9 equations in the system - no other results are reported for his general model). The most important specification differences between the model developed in this research and the models of Backus & Purvis and Owen are the adoption of different asset classifications and the modelling of consumption. In both Backus & Purvis and Owen the consumption function is introduced in the short run specification as outlined in chapter 3 (equation [3.12]). Therefore consumption is measured in level terms in the short run, an approach which has a number of drawbacks. Firstly it is not easy to obtain the long run properties implied by the short run model (by Bewley reparametisation - see below - or other methods). Secondly there are estimation implications arising from the different orders of integration of variables in the short run consumption function - discussed in the section on cointegration later in this chapter. In the model developed in this research the level of desired (real) consumption is specified in the long run model with the change in (real) consumption modelled in the short run.

We now turn to examine how far it is possible to derive the long run coefficients. The matrix of coefficients B_3 do not give the long run responses to the vector of variables, x_t , as B_3 is a combination of long run and dynamic adjustment parameters. One method of obtaining the long run parameters, K , is to reparametise equation [6.4] so that the long run coefficients are directly estimable (Bewley, (1979)). In the case of equation [6.4] reparametisation involves the pre-multiplication of equation [6.4] by B_1^{-1}, which gives :

$$B_1^{-1} \Delta a_t = -a_{t-1} + B_1^{-1}B_2 \Delta x_t + B_1^{-1}B_3 x_{t-1} + B_1^{-1}u_t$$

Now as defined earlier B_3 = B_1K, which simplifies the above to :

$$B_1^{-1} \Delta a_t = -a_{t-1} + B_1^{-1}B_2 \Delta x_t + K x_{t-1} + B_1^{-1}u_t$$

Defining a new matrix F such that B_1^{-1} = I - F where I is an identity matrix , and letting G_1 = $B_1^{-1}B_2$ this equation simplifies to :

$$a_t = F \Delta a_t + G_1 \Delta x_t + K x_{t-1} + B_1^{-1}u_t \qquad [6.6]$$

Thus the long run parameters, K, can be obtained directly from estimation of equation [6.6]. However because the error structure of [6.6] is different to that of equation [6.4] then direct estimation of equation [6.6] would yield different estimates of K than those implied in an estimated equation [6.4]. Therefore to achieve equivalence an instrumental variables technique such as two stage least squares (2SLS) is required. The instruments for Δa_t in equation [6.6] are the estimated values for Δa_t from equation [6.4][1].

Therefore using the conventional approach, estimation of [6.4] yields the short run parameters and estimation of [6.6] provides the long run parameters.

The restrictions of homogeneity and symmetry can then be easily tested in the short run model given by equation [6.4]. The short run homogeneity restriction requires that the coefficients on the interest rate change variables (Δx) sum to zero within an equation (in matrix notation, $B_2 i = 0$). Long run interest rate homogeneity can be imposed by setting $B_1 i = 0$ in [6.4]. Symmetry of interest rate responses can be easily imposed on the short run model, however it is not possible to apply the the symmetry restriction to the long run interest rate parameters implied in equation [6.4] or in the Bewley reparametised equation [6.6] - see Hood (1987) for more discussion.

Before this conventional approach is compared to the cointegration approach the main features of cointegration analysis will be outlined and its application to the model proposed in this research discussed.

6.4 Cointegration

A stationary time series is said to be integrated of order zero and is denoted I(0). A time series, x_t , is said to be I(d) if we have to difference x_t d times before it becomes stationary or I(0). Further, if we consider two series x_t and y_t each of which is I(1) and we can discover a constant, λ, such that:

$$z_t = y_t - \lambda x_t \qquad [6.7]$$

and z_t is I(0) then x_t and y_t are said to be cointegrated and λ is termed the cointegrating factor[2]. A widely adopted interpretation of z_t can be seen from considering the relationship:

$$y_t = \lambda x_t \qquad\qquad [6.8]$$

as the long run or equilibrium relationship. Therefore z_t given by [6.7] measures the gap between the current and equilibrium values of x_t and y_t (sometimes referred to as the equilibrium error). The term equilibrium simply means that there are forces in the economy which make the series x_t and y_t move together in the long run. A necessary condition for equilibrium to hold then is if x_t and y_t are I(1) then z_t must be I(0). If z_t is not I(0) then x_t and y_t will drift apart without bound.

A further result provided by Granger (1983) and Engle and Granger (1987) is that if x_t and y_t are cointegrated then there exists a valid error-correction representation of the data :

$$\Delta x_t = -\rho_1 z_{t-1} + \text{lagged}(\Delta x_t, \Delta y_t) + d(L)\epsilon_{1t} \qquad [6.9]$$

$$\Delta y_t = -\rho_1 z_{t-1} + \text{lagged}(\Delta x_t, \Delta y_t) + d(L)\epsilon_{1t} \qquad [6.10]$$

where ϵ_{1t} , ϵ_{2t} are joint white noise, possibly contemporaneously correlated and with $|\rho_1| + |\rho_2| \neq 0$. The reason for this can be seen when we consider that if x_t and y_t are both I(1) and cointegrated then all the variables in equations [6.9] and [6.10] , changes in x_t , y_t and the lagged equilibrium error z_{t-1}, will be I(0). The above results can be generalised so that x_t represents a vector of time series variables.

The standard interpretation of such models is that in say [6.9] the change in x_t is due to 'short run' effects from lagged values of the change in x_t and y_t and to last periods error (based on the cointegrating or long run regression) which represents the 'long run' adjustment to past equilibrium. Error correction models have become increasingly popular models of dynamic adjustment of variables since the work of Davidson, Hendry, Srba and Yeo (1978) and Hendry and Ungern-Sternberg (1981) on the consumption function. Although the error correction model was first introduced by Phillips (1954) and first used by Sargan (1964). Cointegration provides a theoretical basis for error correction models.

Cointegration analysis as outlined above can be related to this research by considering the generalised error feedback version of the general form of the model [6.3] as outlined earlier in this chapter ie.

$$\Delta a_t = D^{-1}(D_1 + C_3) \Delta a^*_t + D^{-1}D_1 (a^*_{t-1} - a_{t-1}) \qquad [6.3]$$

Letting $\pi = D^{-1}(D_1 + C_3)$ and $L = D^{-1}D_1$ we can rewrite [6.3] as :

$$\Delta a_t = \pi \Delta a^*_t + L (a-a^*)_{t-1} \qquad [6.11]$$

where $(a-a^*)_{t-1}$ is the lagged equilibrium error (ie z_{t-1})

Engle and Granger (1987) propose a two step estimation procedure which allows for explicit testing of the underlying assumption of cointegration. The first step involves estimation of the cointegration regression [6.8], which is the long run model, [6.1], :

$$a^*_t = Kx_t \qquad [6.1]$$

This allows the hypothesis of cointegration to be tested statistically by testing whether the residuals are I(0) or I(1). The residuals from this regression (representing the equilibrium error z_t) are then entered into the error correction model in place of the levels terms.

The advantages of the cointegration approach are first, symmetry and homogeneity restrictions can be easily imposed on the long run parameters. This was not the case for the conventional approach. It can be argued that these restrictions are more likely to apply in the long run than the short run where households are unlikely to have fully adjusted to shocks in the system. This is an important argument in favour of adopting the cointegration approach. Second, the cointegration approach ensures that the long run solution yields a cointegrating vector. Third, simplification of the dynamic equations using the conventional approach, implicitly alters the long run solution. In contrast, with the cointegration approach, the long run parameters are held fixed whilst simplification of the dynamic equations takes place to yield a parsimonious set of equations.

There are also disadvantages with the cointegration approach. Whilst the estimates of the cointegrating regression are consistent they are subject to small sample bias. This appears to lead to an inferior fit in the second stage of the approach. The advantage of being able to impose restrictions on the long run parameters therefore has a trade off in terms of a poor fit of the final dynamic equations. Second, cointegration can be applied to the general form of the model estimated however the partial adjustment model (equation [6.5] cannot be reparametised as an error correction type model. This is not too much of a problem given the advantages of the more general dynamic model when restrictions are tested for, as mentioned earlier.

Therefore on balance the cointegration approach has a number of important advantages over the conventional approach, in particular when estimating heavily parametised systems of equations where the imposition of restrictions on both the long and short run parameters can significantly "improve" the model. Therefore the cointegration approach is adopted in this research and the results of this analysis are reported in the next section.

6.5 Specification of the model

The vector of long run dependent variables, a^*_t , as defined in chapter 4 is :

[CON/P, TRS/P, BTD/P, BSD/P, NATSAV/P, PSD/P, DWE/P, CD/P, -LHP/P, -CONCR/P]

Note that liabilities are entered as negative to satisfy the adding up constraint :

$$\Sigma a^*_t = NW/P + CON/P \qquad [6.12]$$

where NW = net wealth

We can rewrite [6.12] as :

$$\Sigma a^*_t = (NW/P)_{-1} + \Delta(NW/P) + CON/P \qquad [6.13]$$

Now, $\quad \Delta(NW/P) = S/P + CG/P \qquad\qquad\qquad [6.14]$

where S = savings and CG = capital gain accruing to assets subject to price change.

Thus $\qquad \Sigma a^*_t = (NW/P)_{-1} + S/P + CG/P + CON/P \quad [6.15]$

Further, $\quad Y/P = S/P + CON/P \qquad\qquad\qquad [6.16]$

where Y = income. Therefore we can write the long run adding up constraint as:

$$\Sigma a^*_t = (NW/P)_{-1} + CG/P + Y/P \qquad [6.17]$$

Thus the allocated variable in the long run model is separated into (lagged) net wealth, capital gains and income. This makes the model easier to interpret and more comparable with similar models of personal sector financial behaviour. There is also some justification for splitting the allocated variable into existing wealth and new funds as the latter item is clearly less costly to allocate (as discussed in chapter 3, section 3.2). The capital gain component is further dis-aggregrated into gains accruing to dwellings, public sector debt and consumer durables - as discussed in chapter 4 - in order to determine the separate effects of each. Further to this, capital gains on dwellings and consumer dura-bles are split into expected and unexpected components with the expected components representing proxies for the rate of return on dwellings and consumer durables. In order to simplify the estimation process the unexpect-ed component of capital gains is assumed to affect only the asset to which it relates in the period of accrual (the unexpected component is available for re-allocation in the time period after accrual through the lagged net wealth term). Therefore in order to satisfy this and the requirement of adding up, the coefficient on the unexpected component of capital gains is set to one in the asset to which it accrues and zero elsewhere. The adding up constraint of [6.17] therefore becomes:

$$\Sigma a^*_t = (NW/P)_{-1} + Y/P + CGPSD/P + ECGDWE/P \\ + UCGDWE/P + ECGCD/P + UCGCD/P \quad [6.18]$$

The vector of variables determining a^*_t, that is x_t, is :

[PE, RBTD, RBSD, RNATSAV, RPSD, RLHP, RCONCR, $(NW/P)_{-1}$, Y/P, CGPSD/P, ECGDWE/P, UCGDWE/P, ECGCD/P, UCGCD, EQUITY, LAPF, LVR, DUMMY, TREND]

These variables are defined in chapter 4 and above.

In the dynamic model the adding up constraint is given by :

$$\Sigma a_t = (NW/P)_{-1} + (Y/P) + (CGPSD/P) + (ECGDWE/P) \\ + (UCGDWE/P) + (ECGCD/P) + (UCGCD/P) \quad [6.19]$$

Also included in each equation of the model is a constant term, C, and seasonal dummies S_i (i=1,2,3).

The Granger-Engle two step approach to estimation was applied to the model just described and the results are presented and discussed in section 6.8 onwards. Before this, in the next two sections, some practical issues impinging on the estimation, testing and interpretation of the model will be considered.

6.6 Imposing and testing restrictions in estimation

It is assumed that symmetry of interest rate responses applies to the financial asset categories of transaction stocks (TRS), bank time deposits (BTD), building society deposits (BSD), National Savings instruments (NATSAV) and public sector debt. This assumption can of course be tested as discussed later in this section. It was mentioned in chapter four that the negative of the (expected) inflation rate (PE) is the real rate of interest (or cost of holding transaction stock) on the non-interest earning transaction stock (TRS) when real rates of interest are used in the model. Therefore when homogeneity of interest rates is imposed on the model, the coefficient on -PE is included.

Homogeneity of interest rate responses for the five financial assets is imposed as illustrated below (Ai, Bi, Ci, Di, Ei are coefficients):

	-PE	RBTD	RBSD	RNATSAV	RPSD
TRS	A1	A2	A3	A4	(-A1-A2-A3-A4)
BTD	B1	B2	B3	B4	(-B1-B2-B3-B4)
BSD	C1	C2	C3	C4	(-C1-C2-C3-C4)
NATSAV	D1	D2	D3	D4	(-D1-D2-D3-D4)
PSD	E1	E2	E3	E4	(-E1-E2-E3-E4)

Symmetry (and hence homogeneity) of interest rate responses are imposed as follows:

	-PE	RBTD	RBSD	RNATSAV	RPSD
TRS	A1	A2	A3	A4	(-A1-A2-A3-A4)
BTD	A2	B2	B3	B4	(-A2-B2-B3-B4)
BSD	A3	B3	C3	C4	(-A3-B3-C3-C4)
NATSAV	A4	B4	C4	D4	(-A4-B4-C4-D4)
PSD	(-A1-A2-A3-A4)	(-A2-B2-B3-B4)	(-A3-B3-C3-C4)	(-A4-B4-C4-D4)	[-(A1-A2-A3-A4) -(A2-B2-B3-B4) -(A3-B3-C3-C4) -(A4-B4-C4-D4)]

When testing restrictions on a system of equations the likelihood ratio (LR) test is normally used. However the

LR test is an asymptotic test and there is evidence to suggest that in small samples this test can over - reject the null hypothesis. Various small sample corrections have been suggested, for example Pudney (1981) and Simmons (1980). The correction suggested by Pudney has been widely adopted in both studies of consumer demand systems (Anderson and Blundell, (1983)) and asset demands (Hood (1987) , Barr and Cuthbertson (1989)) and will be used here. However it needs to be noted that adjustments like that proposed by Pudney are approximate and have unknown properties in dynamic systems. They should be used as part of a sensitivity analysis to provide an indication of the robustness of the test results.

The adjusted LR statistic is given by :

$$ALR = 2(L_1 - L_0) + nT \ln[(nT - p_1)/(nT - p_0)]$$

where L_1 = log of likelihood function (unconstrained model)

L_0 = log of likelihood function (constrained model)

n = number of equations

T = number of observations

p_1 = number of parameters in unconstrained model

p_0 = number of parameters in constrained model

H_0 : restrictions are acceptable

The critical value for this test is χ^2 with degrees of free dom equal to the number of independent restrictions

Pudney also suggested upward adjustment of the critical value as a further guard against the wrong rejection of the null hypothesis. One of these adjustments is :

$$c_2 = c_1[T/(T-p_1/n)]$$

where c_1 = the critical value from the tables

When cross equation restrictions such as symmetry are imposed then a systems estimator such as Full Information Maximum Likelihood (FIML) is needed in order to satisfy the adding up conditions. When estimating the unrestricted model using FIML in order to obtain the log of the likelihood function to enable a test of the restrictions using an ALR test, then due to singularity of the variance-covariance matrix of the contemporaneous disturbance terms, one of the equations in the system has to be deleted prior to estimation. This is a well documented area - see for example, Barten (1969) and Anderson and Blundell (1982). The FIML estimates are invariant to the deleted equation and the deleted equation coefficients can be recovered using the adding up condition, or if standard errors on the coefficients of the deleted equation are required then the system can be re-estimated with a different equation deleted.

6.7 Expected signs on coefficients

It is generally assumed that financial assets are gross substitutes. Therefore it is expected that own interest rates will be positive and cross interest rates negative. If liabilities are taken to be negative assets similar results will be expected (ie. own rate positive implying that as the interest rate increases, borrowing reduces). However this is not a requirement of utility maximisation and complementary asset categories can exist if there are strong negative covariances of yield or if there are strong income and wealth effects of yield changes. If expected capital gains on consumer durables and dwellings are acting as proxies for returns on these two assets then again positive signs will be expected.

It is useful to note here that a potential problem with estimating portfolio models, analysed by Green and Kiernan (1989), is that a combination of measurement error in the data and multicollinearity can lead to (i) own rate coefficients which are likely to be of correct sign but an under-estimate of the true value and (ii) cross rate coefficients that are small in size and in fact may be so small in relation to the true parameter as to be wrongly signed on "a priori" grounds.

6.8 Application of the cointegration approach

Before the Granger-Engle two step procedure is carried out it is necessary first to test for the order of integration of the variables in the long run or cointegrating regression [6.1].

There are various tests proposed for testing for the order of integration of a time series. Here the Augmented Dickey-Fuller (ADF) test for unit roots is used. Thus the following auxiliary regressions are run:

$$\Delta x_t = \beta_0 + \beta_1 x_{t-1} + \Sigma_i \ \gamma_i \Delta x_{t-i} + \epsilon_t$$

H_0: x_t is distributed as I(1)
H_a: x_t is distributed as I(0)

$$\Delta^2 x_t = \beta_0 + \beta_1 \Delta x_{t-1} + \Sigma_i \ \gamma_i \Delta^2 x_{t-i} + \epsilon_t$$

H_0: Δx_t is distributed as I(1)
H_a: Δx_t is distributed as I(0)

where the test statistic is the t statistic on β_1

Critical values are for the test statistic are not standard and are given in Fuller [(1976, Table 8.5.2) for the regression with an intercept (ie. those critical values labelled τ_μ in table 8.5.2)].

A problem with using the ADF test is determining the value of the lag length i. Too low a value leads to invalid statistics due to autocorrelation remaining in the residuals, too high a value results in loss of power in the test. One solution suggested by Engle and Yoo (1987) is to select i using one of the model selection tests based on some model selection criteria. Yi and Judge (1988) compare a number of such criteria and find the Schwartz criteria to be superior in that it reaches a well defined global minima with a fairly parsimonious parametisation[3]. Webb (1988) in a study of commodity prices also uses the Schwartz criteria in this respect.

The ADF statistics calculated in this study are also undertaken using the Schwartz criteria to determine the appropriate lag length. The results of the ADF test for the variables in the long run model are given in the table below.

Table 6.1
Augmented Dickey Fuller (ADF) test results for levels and changes in the variables

Variable	ADF	Variable	ADF
CON	0.21	CON	-3.79
TRS	-1.73	TRS	-4.47
BTD	-2.54	BTD	-3.87
BSD	1.32	BSD	-3.32
NATSAV	0.10	NATSAV	-4.61
PSD	-0.20	PSD	-5.16
DWE	-0.84	DWE	-2.72
CD	-1.35	CD	-4.65
LHP	1.23	LHP	-2.98
CONCR	0.29	CONCR	-2.93
NW	2.03	DNW	-2.96
Y	-1.41	Y	-4.69
CGPSD	-1.01	CGPSD	-4.21
PE	-1.63	PE	-3.07
CGDWE	-0.89	CGDWE	-5.32
CGCD	0.42	CGCD	-3.12
RBTD	-1.10	RBTD	-5.25
RBSD	-1.08	RBSD	-4.10
RNATSAV	-1.83	RNATSAV	-4.44
RPSD	-1.74	RPSD	-4.66
RLHP	-0.79	RLHP	-4.07
RCONCR	-1.04	RCONCR	-5.45
EQUITY	-1.53	EQUITY	-4.67
LAPF	2.61	LAPF	-3.27
LVR	-1.00	LVR	-4.81

The critical values for the above ADF statistics are approximately -2.93 at the 5% level and -3.58 at the 1% level.

The left hand side results for levels of the variables in the long run equations are all lower than the critical value and therefore fail to reject the null hypothesis, thus implying that the variables in levels are I(1) processes. The right hand set of results for differences of the variables are almost all greater than the critical value for the test. The only problematic variable is ΔDWE although this is very close to the 5% critical value and we can therefore conclude that the differenced variables are stationary or I(0), implying that before differencing they were I(1).

The next stage of the Granger-Engle two step estimation procedure is to estimate the cointegration regression equations [6.1] and then test the order of integration of the residuals (z_t). These should of course be I(0).

The estimation period, as stated in chapter 5, runs from 1976 Q1 to 1987 Q4. In the early attempts to estimate the model it became clear that the colinearity problem was particularly severe when all 6 interest rates are included in each equation. As would be expected the correlation between RCONCR and RBTD and between RBSD and RLHP was very high. After a number of experiments it was therefore decided that (i) the rates of interest on the 2 liabilities, RCONCR and RLHP, would be omitted from the financial asset equations (TRS, BTD, BSD, NATSAV, PSD) (ii) the loan to value ratio (LVR) is omitted from TRS, BTD, BSD, NATSAV and PSD for the same reason (iii) RBTD, RBSD, RNATSAV and RPSD are omitted from those equations where RCONCR and RLHP were expected to play a significant role (CON, CD, DWE, LHP, CONCR). It was also decided to omit the expected inflation variable (PE) from all but the five financial asset equations. It was argued in chapter four that expected inflation is included to pick up the shift out of transaction stocks when inflation is rising, and it can be further argued that this shift is most likely to be to other financial assets. In order to impose the adding up constraint for the model which includes these zero restrictions the unrestricted estimation has also to be undertaken using a system estimation method such as maximum likelihood.

To summarise again the specification of the long run model in this study:

$$a^* = C + b_1Y + b_2NW_{-1} + b_3EQUITY + b_4LAPF +$$
$$b_5CGPSD + b_6ECGDWE + b_7ECGCD + b_8RBTD +$$
$$b_9RBSD + b_{10}RNATSAV + b_{11}RPSD +$$
$$b_{12}RCONCR + b_{13}RLHP + b_{14}PE + b_{15}LVR +$$
$$b_{16}TREND + b_{17}DUMMY + b_{18}S1 + b_{19}S2 +$$
$$b_{20}S3 + b_{21}UCGDWE + b_{22}UCGCD$$

where a^* is defined as :

[CON/P, TRS/P, BTD/P, BSD/P, NATSAV/P, PSD/P, DWE/P, CD/P, -LHP/P, -CONCR/P]

The following table shows some summary statistics for the cointegrating regressions - the coefficient values for these regressions are shown in table 1 in appendix 6A, and discussed in the next section.

Table 6.2
Durbin Watson (DW) and augmented Dickey Fuller
statistics for the cointegrating regressions

Equation	CRDW	ADF	
CON	1.54	-6.72	
TRS	1.32	-5.97	$H_0 : z_t$ dist. I(1)
BTD	1.46	-5.41	
BSD	1.32	-5.03	
NATSAV	0.88	-5.26	Critical values
PSD	1.27	-5.38	(approx)
DWE	1.56	-5.67	
CD	1.45	-5.10	5%: -2.93
LHP	1.55	-4.98	1%: -3.58
CONCR	1.30	-5.42	

The first point to note about the results in table 6.2 is that the ADF statistics for the residuals are all greater than the 5% critical value (thus rejecting the null and hence the residuals are I(0)). A second test for cointegration - the cointegrating regression Durbin Watson test (CRDW) - is based upon the work of Sargan and Bhargava (1983) and has a null hypothesis of no cointegration. For cointegration the DW statistic in the cointegrating regression should not be too low. Critical values have been provided by Engle and Granger (1987) (the 3 variable values are reported in Hall (1986)) but these can only be used as a guide as they are based upon Monte Carlo simulations with 100 observations (only 48 observations were available for the cointegrating regressions above) and have only been calculated for the 2 and 3 variable case.

			1%	5%
2 var	CRDW		0.511	0.386
3 var	CRDW		0.488	0.367

In each of the cointegrating regression equations the DW statistic are comfortably greater than the 3 variable critical values for this test. Thus on the basis of this and the ADF statistics we can conclude that the residuals are likely to be I(0). Hence the variables in each equation form a cointegrating vector.

It is now possible to move to the next stage of the estimation process which is to estimate the system of error correction equations [6.11] with the residuals from the long run model substituted for the equilibrium error terms $(a-a^*)_{t-1}$.

Now as
$$\sum_{i=1}^{k} (a_i - a^*_i)_{t-1} = 0$$

then only k-1 of the equilibrium error terms are required in [6.11]. It is worth noting here that it was found necessary in this study to impose this condition on the model (ie. it is not imposed automatically by the estimation process).

A summary of the specification of the dynamic model in this study is given below :

$$\Delta a = C + e_1 Y + e_2 NW_{-1} + e_3 EQUITY + e_4 LAPF +$$
$$e_5 CGPSD + e_6 ECGDWE + e_7 ECGCD +$$
$$e_8 RBTD + e_9 RBSD + e_{10} RNATSAV + e_{11} RPSD +$$
$$e_{12} RCONCR + e_{13} RLHP + e_{14} PE + e_{15} LVR +$$
$$e_{16} TREND + e_{17} DUMMY + e_{18} S1 + e_{19} S2 +$$
$$e_{20} S3 + e_{21} R_1(-1) + e_{22} R_2(-1) + e_{23} R_3(-1) +$$
$$e_{24} R_4(-1) + e_{25} R_5(-1) + e_{26} R_6(-1) + e_{27} R_7(-1) +$$
$$e_{28} R_8(-1) + e_{29} R_9(-1) + e_{30} UCGDWE +$$
$$e_{31} UCGCD$$

where Δa is defined as :

[$\Delta(CON/P)$, $\Delta(TRS/P)$, $\Delta(BTD/P)$, $\Delta(BSD/P)$, $\Delta(NATSAV/P)$, $\Delta(PSD/P)$, $\Delta(DWE/P)$, $\Delta(CD/P)$, $-\Delta(LHP/P)$, $-\Delta(CONCR/P)$]

and $R_i(-1) = (a_i - a^*_i)_{-1}$

Estimation of the unrestricted version of [6.11] is by maximum likelihood and the results are reported in appendix 6A and discussed below.

6.9 Long run model

6.9.1 Unrestricted results

The first point to note is that no combined role could be found for the variables representing wealth in Life Assurance and Pension Funds (LAPF) and wealth held as company securities (EQUITY). On the basis of an adjusted likelihood ratio test the LAPF variable was dropped and the EQUITY variable kept in the model. Second, there are a large number of coefficient values reported in Appendix 6.A and clearly it is not possible to comment on all of them. In all the discussion that follows it will be the salient points of the reported results that are commented upon.

The signs on the coefficients of the unrestricted long run model are quite good. Correct signs are found on the own interest rates in the bank time deposits (BTD), building society deposits (BSD) and public sector debt

(PSD) equations.

Whilst these unrestricted results are encouraging there is clearly some room for improvement. In particular, the own rate sign in the NATSAV equation would be expected to be positive. Also some of the cross interest rate signs are not what would be expected if the financial assets are viewed as substitutes. For example the sign on rate of interest on national savings in the bank time deposits equation. The next step therefore is to examine the consequences of imposing homogeneity and symmetry on the interest rate coefficients.

6.9.2 Restricted results

Symmetry and homogeneity were imposed on the five financial asset returns as outlined in section 6.6. Several coefficients went very small after the imposition of these restrictions and so were set to zero. These were the rate of interest on national savings in the building time deposits equation, the rate of interest on national savings and bank time deposits in the transaction money equation and the EQUITY variable in the loans for house purchase equation. The adjusted likelihood ratio (ALR) was used to test for these combined restrictions of symmetry, homogeneity and four zero's with the following results.

$$ALR = 36.9$$

critical value = χ^2, (19), (0.05) = 30.1
adjusted critical value = 41.4

Therefore these restrictions are accepted, but only after downward adjustment of the LR statistic and upward adjustment of the critical value. These adjustments, as noted in section 6.6, are commonly used and therefore this result is accepted.

There is an improvement in the long run results after imposing these restrictions as can be seen in Table 2 in appendix 6A. In particular the coefficients on the own interest rates in the five financial asset equations are now of the expected sign and greater in size than the coefficients on the cross rates of interest. The cross interest rate signs almost all imply substitutability between the financial asset categories. The one exception is the positive sign on the rate of return on public sector debt in the bank time deposits equation (and vice versa given symmetry). This suggests complementarity between these two assets. Imposing zero on this coefficient was not accepted using the ALR test. Therefore the traditional notion of strong substitutability between money and bonds is questioned, at least for the Personal sector, by this model. This may be a consequence of the interaction of multicollinearity and measurement error (mentioned earlier in this chapter) However complementarity between bank time deposits and bonds was also found in a similar study of Personal Sector portfolio behaviour by Hood (1987). In this model, it is building society deposits which are seen as the natural short term alternative to long term financial assets represented by bonds. This is not an unreasonable result.

The effects of expected inflation in the long run are now clearer with a definite shift out of transaction money stocks, if inflation is expected to rise, into building society deposits and public sector debt.

The expected (ie. negative) relationship was found between demand for loans for house purchase and the own interest rate. The expected relationship between demand for dwellings and the rate of interest on loans for house purchase was also found. These results suggests that the LVR variable is succeeding in capturing the effect of rationing. This contrasts with Barr and Cuthbertson (1989) who also use an LVR variable to proxy rationing but find they have to set the mortgage interest rate to zero over the period of rationing to obtain the expected sign on the mortgage interest rate in the demand for mortgages equation. The expected (positive) sign was also found on the LVR variable in both the demand for mortgages and the demand for housing equations.

For the other liability modelled, the expected signs are found for the rate of interest on consumer credit in the

the demand equations for consumer credit, consumer durables and consumption. However, these results only occur after setting the rate of interest on consumer credit to zero for the period up to 1983 quarter two. This was rationalised in chapter four, section four by arguing that households only became interest rate sensitive on consumer credit debt after 1983.

Turning now to the results for the effect of expected capital gains on household decisions. It was argued in chapter four that a positive relationship between consumption and expected capital gains would be expected as less saving is required out of income to increase wealth to desired levels. This result is found for all three types of capital gain components identified in the model. It was also argued in chapter four that, for the same reasoning, a negative relationship would be expected between the demand for financial assets and expected capital gains. There is some evidence for this, for example negative signs on the capital gain on consumer durables in the bank and building society deposit equations. However there is also evidence to the contrary with expected capital gains on dwellings having a positive effect on transaction stocks, building society deposits and national savings. This may be explained by reference to the experience over the 1980's whereby large capital gains accrued to housing and a significant part of the resulting equity built up in housing was released, facilitated by the the greater availability of mortgage lending. This equity release from housing however boosted both consumption and financial asset acquisition (whilst the saving ratio was falling). Thus it is quite plausible for expected capital gains on dwellings to have a positive effect on financial asset acquisition. This may imply a desired target for financial asset holdings which is separate from the desired target for total wealth holdings. Equity wealth, which essentially reflects the effects of capital gains accruing to equities held by households, can be seen as a substitute for dwellings wealth and financial wealth held in the form of building society deposits and national savings. Therefore building society deposits again appear to act as a short term alternative to longer term financial assets.

Turning now to the net wealth and income variables the effects of which are seen clearly in table 3 of appendix A which presents the long run elasticities. Net wealth in the long run can be seen to strongly affect real decisions, that is, the acquisition of dwellings and consumer durables and the purchase of consumer non-durables. Related to this is the effect of net wealth on the two liabilities. The two financial assets most strongly affected by net wealth in the long run are bank time and building society deposits.

Looking finally at the results for the dummy and trend variables. The signs on the dummy variable show that it is picking up the effect of the removal of the corset and the general loosening of restrictions on credit which occurred at the beginning of the 1980's decade. Thus the expected signs are found in the dwellings, loans for house purchase and consumer credit equations. The negative sign on the dummy variable in the transactions stock equation may reflect a switch to the use of borrowed funds (credit cards etc.) and away from holding transaction balances to manage spending decisions as a result of innovation and greater availability in relation to short term credit. The trend variable is fulfilling its intended role in picking up the switch out of bank time deposits and into transaction stocks and building society deposits following various innovations over the 1980's including the introduction of current accounts paying interest by both banks and building societies.

Before turning to examine the dynamic model results it is useful to further consider the long run elasticities reported in table 3, appendix 6A, as these provide a means of comparing the results from this model with those of other empirical studies of Personal Sector behaviour and so provide a check on the plausibility of the model. One similar study of Personal Sector portfolio behaviour is that of Barr and Cuthbertson (1989). This study also adopted the Granger-Engle two step approach to estimation and so was also able to impose the restrictions of homogeneity and symmetry on the long run interest rate coefficients. There are no other comparable studies of UK Personal Sector behaviour which report long run elasticities, however there are a few studies of parts of Personal Sector financial decision making which provide long run elasticities. The following table reports selected long run elasticities from these studies and the Barr and Cuthbertson study.

Table 6.3
Long run elasticities obtained from other studies of personal sector behaviour

	PE	RBTD	RBSD	RCONCR	RLHP	W	
M1	-2.9	-1.8	-1.8			-1.4	B&C
BTD	1.9	2.8	0.0			1.8	B&C
BSD	0.2	0.0	0.8			1.6	B&C
LHP					-0.32		W
CD				-0.84			D
CON				-0.49			D

NB. B&C : Barr & Cuthbertson (1989)
   W   : Wilcox (1985)
   D   : Dicks (1988)

The first point to note is that the M1 price and interest rate elasticities in the Barr and Cuthbertson study are considerably larger than those found for the transaction stock (TRS) category in this study. Although there are some minor differences in the construction of the TRS and M1 these cannot explain the extent of the differences. As Barr and Cuthbertson note that their elasticities are consistent with single equation studies of M1 then this suggests problems with the TRS equation in this study and further work is required here. With regard to the own rates on bank time deposits (BTD) and building society deposits (BSD) the own rates in both studies are large although the elasticity for the own rate in BSD in this study is almost twice as big. The wealth elasticities are not really comparable as wealth in the Barr and Cuthbertson study is simply liquid asset wealth. Turning to the elasticity on the own rate for loans for house purchase (LHP). This is broadly the same for this study and the study by Wilcox. The elasticities on the rate on consumer credit in the two consumption demands are considerably larger in the study by Dicks although the relative size of the consumption to consumer durables elasticity is broadly the same for the two studies.

On the basis of this limited comparison with similar empirical studies it is possible to conclude that the elasticities for this study are not too implausible.

6.10 Dynamic model

6.10.1 Unrestricted results

There is less known about the behaviour of agents when out of equilibrium and therefore a priori views on signs on the dynamic model coefficients are less strongly held when compared to the long run coefficients. As a consequence there will be less discussion of individual coefficient results for the dynamic model. The unrestricted dynamic results are shown in tables 4 and 5 in appendix 6.A .

The own and cross interest rate coefficients in the five financial asset equations are not as large in the dynamic model, which is as one would expect. The own rate coefficients on the four financial assets are of the expected sign. Also the sign on expected inflation in the transaction stock equation and the own interest rate coefficients in the two liability equations are of the expected sign. As with the unrestricted long run results there is room for improvement in the cross interest rate coefficients in the financial asset equations and so the restrictions of homogeneity and symmetry are imposed and tested for.

6.10.2 Restricted results

Symmetry and homogeneity were imposed in the same way as for the long run model. With the imposition of these restrictions the coefficients on the rate of interest on bank time deposits in the transaction stock equation and the rate of return on public sector debt in the transaction stock and bank time deposit equations became indistinguishable from zero and so were set to zero. Using the ALR statistic to test for the imposition of symmetry, homogeneity and zero restrictions the following results emerged :

$$ALR = 22.7$$

critical value $= \chi^2 (19),(0.05) = 30.14$

So the combined set of restrictions are accepted without the need for upward adjustment of the critical value.

The restricted dynamic model results are reported in tables 6 and 7 of appendix 6.A . The cross interest rates are largely of the expected sign, if substitutability is expected, and significant. The exceptions are the coefficients on the return on public sector debt in the national savings equation and the return on national savings in the bank time deposits equation which are significant and suggest complementarity. The other interest rate coefficient which has a different sign than would be expected is the rate on consumer credit in the consumption equation. This however is not significant.

The adjustment coefficients (ie. the coefficients on the $(a_i\text{-}a^*_i)$ variables) are shown in table 8 in appendix 6.A . These coefficients are reasonable with all all the own adjustment parameters having the expected negative sign (implying that when the actual stock is different to the desired that short run transactions in the own stock aim to reduce the difference) and all are statistically significant. In addition the majority of the cross adjustment coefficients have the expected positive sign. Very small and insignificant adjustment coefficients have been set to zero (these zero restrictions are easily accepted using an ALR test). The existence of some significant negatively signed cross adjustment coefficients may be accounted for by complementary adjustment paths An example of this is provided by the coefficients on bank time deposits and transaction stocks adjustment in both the bank time deposits and transaction stock equations. Complementary adjustment here is not unreasonable

One interesting result of these adjustment coefficients is the number of different disequilibria of actual from desired asset and liability stocks that dynamic adjustment of consumption depends upon. Normally in modelling consumption disequilibria in single equation studies only a net liquid assets category is allowed for (see chapter three). The results of this study suggest that this is not acceptable as the implication of a net liquid assets disequilibrium is that the dynamic adjustment of consumption has the same relationship to disequilibrium in the different components of net liquid assets. This can be seen from the results in table 7 to be not the case. Also, the dynamic adjustment of consumption can be seen to depend on disequilibria in illiquid and physical assets (ie. a wider set of assets than implied by the use of net liquid assets).

6.10.3 Model evaluation

There are various ways in which econometric models can be evaluated and three methods often used are:

i)   Comparison with Time Series models
ii)   Ex post forecasts
iii)   Ex ante forecasts

The last two of these methods can be further separated into forecasts made within the sample period and forecasts outside the sample period. The first method will not be considered here except where the model forecasts are compared to the alternative of a no change forecast in the construction of the Theil inequality statistic (discussed later). Fair (1986) identifies two problems when ex ante forecasts are used in model evaluation. The first is that ex ante forecasts are based on guessed rather than actual values of the exogenous variables. Therefore errors in the forecasted endogenous variables will be attributable to bad guesses as well as problems with the model and it is not possible to isolate the errors due to the model. The second problem is that generally subjective adjustments are made to ex ante model forecasts and so evaluation of these forecasts is an evaluation of the forecasting performance of the model builder rather than the model. Therefore ex post forecasts were used in evaluating the model in this research although because of the shortage of degrees of freedom in estimating such a heavily parametised model it was not possible to save some data for the use of outside sample evaluation. Thus the ex post evaluation is a within sample tracking exercise and is therefore open to the criticism of the possible existence of data mining. That is the model chosen may provide the best fit over the estimation period but may be a poor representation of the true structure. Within sample evaluation will not discover this, whereas outside sample evaluation should and so the evaluation results discussed in this section should be viewed with this potential problem in mind.

Before examining the results of the tracking exercise some diagnostic statistics for the model, shown in table 9 in appendix 6.A, will be considered. The coefficients of determination are reasonable for systems estimation of financial asset type equations and given that one of the costs of the two step approach to estimation, as mentioned earlier in this chapter is a poorer fit for the dynamic equations.

The Box-Pierce (B-P) statistics for serial correlation up to order 8, whilst not conclusive given the nature of the test, do not suggest serious mis-specification in any of the equations. The consumption and bank time deposits equations have B-P statistics which exceed the 5% significance level but which just fall below the 1% level. It is useful to note that when the dummy variable is dropped from the model then the B-P statistics (not reported) show severe mis-specification in the national savings and loans for house purchase equations. This result provides additional support for the use of the dummy variable.

Summary statistics of the tracking errors for the dependent variables from a static simulation of the model over the full estimation period using the actual exogenous variables are reported in table 10 in appendix 6A. The statistics reported which compare actual and predicted values of the dependent variables (P_i and A_i refer to predicted and actual values respectively) are :

(i) root mean square error (RMSE)
$$= [\Sigma(P_i - A_i)^2/n]^{\frac{1}{2}}$$

(ii) mean absolute error (MAS)
$$= [\Sigma|P_i - A_i|/n]$$

(iii) mean error (ME)
$$= [\Sigma(P_i - A_i/n]$$

(iv) Theil inequality statistic (U)
$$= [\Sigma(P_i - A_i)^2/\Sigma A_i^2]$$

The mean error (ME) statistic can be quite small due to positive and negative errors offsetting each other by chance. Therefore less attention should be paid to this. The mean absolute error (MAS) measure penalises large errors less than does the root mean square error. The Theil inequality statistic (U) has a minimum value of zero but no upper limit. However a U statistic less than 1 is desirable as this implies that the model predictions are better (have lower errors) than a naive forecast of no change. With these qualifications in mind it can be seen that the tracking performance of the model largely reflects the diagnostic statistics discussed earlier. Plots of actual with predicted values for the real stocks of assets and consumption are also shown in appendix 6.B . The predicted values here are derived by cumulatively adding the predicted changes to starting values (ie. at 1976 Q1) for the asset stock or consumption.

For comparison a dynamic in-sample simulation was run over the same period as the static, thus allowing errors to cumulate by feeding in the predicted values of lagged variables (the adjustment parameters in this model). Plots of actual with predicted are again shown in appendix 6B.

The dynamic tracking results are quite encouraging with little evidence of explosive divergence in any equation. This is clearly due to the error-correction specification of the model. There is however some concern with the tracking performance of the bank time deposits, national savings, public sector debt and loans for house purchase equations over the last few quarters of the period tracked. This will need further investigation as more data becomes available.

6.11 Conclusion

A number of conclusions emerge from this discussion of the estimated model. The use of the Granger-Engle two step approach to estimation is supported in this type of study as in particular it has enabled plausible long run or desired parameters to be estimated before the search for a parsimonious system of dynamic equations takes place. The two step procedure plus the imposition of the restrictions of symmetry and homogeneity have enabled largely well determined and correctly signed coefficients to be estimated thus overcoming the problems found by previous researchers in this area in particular where attempts have been made to estimate an integrated type model. Most importantly for this study the results provide encouragement for the use of an integrated approach to modelling household expenditure and financial decisions. Many examples of relationships have been found which are excluded when separability is assumed. For example a complex pattern of relationships has been found in this study between capital uncertain assets such as public sector debt and equity and capital certain assets. Public sector debt appears to be complementary to some parts of capital certain assets (bank time deposits) and substitutable to other parts (building society deposits and national savings). Similar results are found for equity where again it is found to be complementary with bank time deposits and substitutable with building society deposits and national savings. With separate modelling of capital uncertain and capital certain assets complementarity or substitutability can only be allowed for between say, public sector debt and the whole of capital certain assets. In addition, although many routes for influence between liabilities, real assets, financial assets and consumption had to be ruled in this study because of the problems of multicollinearity there are still a number of interesting relationships revealed. For example there is some evidence to support the hypothesis of substitutability between real assets and a wide variety of financial assets. This is clear for the case of consumer durables which is shown to be a substitute to all assets other than transaction stocks. However the position is not as straightforward for dwellings as the build up of equity in this asset and the greater availability of credit to release these gains has permitted financial asset acquisition alongside investment in housing and thus a complementary relationship between dwellings and most financial assets. This evidence of substitutability between real assets and most financial assets tends to support the monetarist version of the portfolio balance transmission mechanism whereby asset holders who find their portfolios in imbalance because of a surplus of money are just as likely to switch directly into real and long term financial assets as they are into shorter term financial assets. Further relationships between the various expenditure and financial decisions of households are evidenced through the cross adjustment parameters.

In general the long run results appear more plausible than the dynamic results. This is perhaps to be expected because in the short run households are adjusting to shocks. Another encouraging result of the model is the strong interest rate effects found for financial assets which are broadly comparable with the results of another recent study of personal sector portfolio behaviour.

In overall conclusion the model developed in this study, in comparison to similar but separable studies, has provided additional insight into the relationships between real and financial decisions of the personal sector. However there is still further scope provided by the integrated framework for investigating such relationships. To extend the scope of this type of model though, for example by including all rates of return in each equation, would require consideration of ways of minimising the effects of multicollinearity that would occur. Further work on the model suggested by the discussion above would include a wider examination of the restrictions of symmetry and homogeneity. It may be possible to include both real rates of return and rates of interest on liabilities in the symmetric matrix. Further improvements may be achieved by the adoption of the AIDS framework specified in levels, which is more suited to modelling systems of demand equations and imposing restrictions.

In the next chapter the preferred model resulting from the estimation process is used to to undertake policy simulations. These simulation experiments provide an opportunity to further examine some of the real and financial inter-linkages highlighted in the above discussion of the estimation results.

Notes

1. To see that error structure of [6.6] estimated using 2SLS is the same as the error structure of [6.4] then writing the estimated values of Δa_t in [6.4] as $\Delta \hat{a}_t$, it follows that :

$$\Delta a_t = \Delta \hat{a}_t + u_t$$

Substituting this into equation [6.6] gives :

$$at = F\ (\Delta \hat{a}_t + u_t) + G_1\ \Delta x_t + K\ x_{t-1} + B_1^{-1} u_t$$

Since $F = I - B_1^{-1}$ then this simplifies to :

$$at = F\ \Delta \hat{a}_t + G_1\ \Delta x_t + k\ x_{t-1} + u_t$$

2. It can be noted that a model of the form:

$$y_t = x_t + e_t$$

135

where y_t is I(0) and x_t is I(1) makes no sense because of the differing temporal properties of x_t and y_t. For this model the only theoretically plausible value for is zero.

3. The Schwarz Criterion is given by

$$S = n \log \sigma^2 + q \log n$$

where n is the number of degrees of freedom, q is the number of parameters estimated and σ^2 is the residual variance (square of the standard error of the regression)

Appendix 6A
Estimation results

This appendix contains the tables showing estimation results referred to in chapter 6. The following notes apply:

(i)   t statistics are shown in parentheses

(ii)   0.0 indicates an imposed coefficient of zero

(iii)   * implies the coefficient has been obtained from the 'adding up' constraint

Long run coefficients - unrestricted model

	-PE	RBTD	RBSD	RNATSAV	RPSD	RCONCR	RLHP	LVR
CON	0.0	0.0	0.0	0.0	0.0	0.02	0.0	0.0
TRS	0.83	0.18	-0.54	-0.49	-0.10	0.0	0.0	0.0
BTD	-0.60	0.42	-0.53	0.39	0.27	0.0	0.0	0.0
BSD	0.56	-0.26	0.37	-0.24	-0.23	0.0	0.0	0.0
NATSAV	0.38	-0.12	0.27	-0.12	-0.09	0.0	0.0	0.0
PSD	-0.57	-0.23	0.43	0.46	0.14	0.0	0.0	0.0
DWE	0.0	0.0	0.0	0.0	0.0	0.0	-0.25	0.19
CD	0.0	0.0	0.0	0.0	0.0	-0.06	0.0	0.0
-CONCR	0.0	0.0	0.0	0.0	0.0	0.04	0.0	0.0
-LHP	0.0	0.0	0.0	0.0	0.0	0.0	0.25	-0.19

	EQUITY	CGDWE	CGCD	CGPSD	NW_{-1}	Y	DUMMY *100	TREND *100
CON	-0.000	0.032	0.002	0.01	0.029	0.03	0.39	0.06
TRS	0.038	0.016	0.312	-0.11	0.007	0.07	-2.66	0.45
BTD	0.004	0.003	-0.259	0.21	0.021	0.05	3.35	-0.41
BSD	-0.009	0.060	-0.211	0.09	0.031	0.31	-0.91	1.93
NATSAV	-0.024	0.028	-0.165	0.13	0.006	0.01	0.03	0.40
PSD	0.018	0.044	-0.053	0.53	-0.001	0.03	-0.26	0.19
DWE	-0.087	0.874	-1.350	1.22	0.887	0.31	8.59	0.96
CD	0.046	0.186	1.693	-0.02	0.125	0.26	-3.11	-0.86
-CONCR	0.016	-0.088	0.353	-0.31	-0.032	-0.02	-2.42	-0.49
-LHP	-0.004	-0.155	-0.679	-0.76	-0.075	-0.04	-2.99	-2.23

NB: Standard errors of the cointegrating regression are inconsistent and therefore no t statistics are reported.

Table 6A.2
Long run coefficients - restricted model (symmetry imposed on -PE, RBTD,RBSD,RNATSAV,RPSD)

	-PE	RBTD	RBSD	RNATSAV	RPSD	RCONCR	RLHP	LVR
CON	0.0	0.0	0.0	0.0	0.0	-0.02	0.0	0.0
TRS	0.09	0.0	-0.06	0.0	-0.03	0.0	0.0	0.0
BTD	0.0	0.51	-0.49	-0.13	0.11	0.0	0.0	0.0
BSD	-0.06	-0.49	0.73	0.0	-0.18	0.0	0.0	0.0
NATSAV	0.0	-0.13	0.0	0.15	-0.02	0.0	0.0	0.0
PSD	-0.03	0.11	-0.18	-0.02	0.12	0.0	0.0	0.0
DWE	0.0	0.0	0.0	0.0	0.0	0.0	-0.24	0.34
CD	0.0	0.0	0.0	0.0	0.0	-0.02	0.0	0.0
-CONCR	0.0	0.0	0.0	0.0	0.0	0.04	0.0	0.0
-LHP	0.0	0.0	0.0	0.0	0.0	0.0	0.24	-0.34

	EQUITY	CGDWE	CGCD	CGPSD	NW_{-1}	Y	DUMMY *100.0.0	TREND *100
CON	-0.005	0.061	0.015	0.06	0.059	0.06	1.16	0.11
TRS	0.043	0.060	0.324	-0.27	0.002	0.04	-3.18	0.52
BTD	0.016	-0.053	-0.402	0.21	0.021	0.02	2.92	-0.46
BSD	-0.013	0.141	-0.178	0.09	0.024	0.34	0.28	1.99
NATSAV	-0.037	0.108	-0.062	0.25	0.002	0.09	2.06	0.47
PSD	0.018	0.038	-0.022	0.76	0.002	0.09	1.25	0.17
DWE	-0.078	1.079	-1.260	1.35	0.864	0.45	12.86	1.08
CD	0.016	0.161	1.703	0.12	0.143	0.30	-2.34	-0.88
-CONCR	0.040	-0.184	0.316	-0.52	-0.029	-0.13	-5.81	-0.62
-LHP	0.0	-0.407	-0.567	-1.03	-0.052	-0.25	-9.21	-2.39

Long run elasticities

	PE	RBTD	RBSD	RNATSAV	RPSD	RCONCR	RLHP
TRS	-0.32	0.0	-0.21	0.0	-0.11		
BTD	0.0	2.29	-2.22	-0.59	0.49		
BSD	0.12	-1.01	1.50	0.0	-0.37		
NATSAV	0.0	-1.18	0.0	1.36	-0.18		
PSD	-0.23	0.84	-1.37	-0.15	0.92		
CON						-0.06	0.0
DWE						0.0	-0.08
CD						-0.02	0.0
CONCR						-0.16	0.0
LHP						0.0	-0.36

	Y	NW
TRS	0.03	0.05
BTD	0.39	0.03
BSD	0.20	0.23
NATSAV	0.07	0.26
PSD	0.06	0.22
CON	0.75	0.06
DWE	1.17	0.05
CD	0.78	0.13
CONCR	0.55	0.19
LHP	0.33	0.12

NB. Interest rate elasticities are semi-elasticities
(ie. $100(da/a/dX)$ where X=interest rate and a=asset evaluated
at sample mean)

Wealth elasticities calculated using: $(da/a)/(dNW/NW)$
(where a=asset value, NW=net wealth - both evaluated at sample
mean)

Dynamic coefficients - unrestricted model

	-ΔPE	ΔRBTD	ΔRBSD	ΔRNATSAV	ΔRPSD	ΔRCONCR	ΔRLHP
ΔCON	0.0	0.0	0.0	0.0	0.0	0.06 (0.6)	0.0
ΔTRS	0.20 (1.7)	-0.03 (0.2)	0.03 (0.3)	-0.18 (-1.4)	-0.03 (-0.7)	0.0	0.0
ΔBTD	0.14 (1.2)	0.15 (2.6)	-0.39 (-4.3)	0.30 (2.6)	0.02 (0.8)	0.0	0.0
ΔBSD	-0.76 (-4.4)	0.01 (0.2)	0.37 (2.7)	0.32 (1.7)	-0.05 (-1.4)	0.0	0.0
ΔNATSAV	0.01 (0.1)	0.01 (1.1)	-0.12 (-2.9)	0.07 (1.3)	0.03 (2.1)	0.0	0.0
ΔPSD	0.41 (2.7)	-0.14 (-1.9)	0.11 (1.1)	-0.50 (-3.6)	0.03 (1.0)	0.0	0.0
ΔDWE	0.0	0.0	0.0	0.0	0.0	0.0	-0.07 (-1.1)
ΔCD	0.0	0.0	0.0	0.0	0.0	-0.09 (-2.7)	0.0
-ΔCONCR	0.0	0.0	0.0	0.0	0.0	0.03 (0.7)	0.0
-ΔLHP	0.0	0.0	0.0	0.0	0.0	0.0	0.07 (1.9)

	ΔLVR	ΔEQ	ΔNW$_{-1}$	ΔY	ΔCGDWE	ΔCGCD	ΔCGPSD	D	T
ΔCON	0.0	-0.014	0.018	0.03	0.014	0.069	-0.002	-0.01	0.01
		(-2.8)	(3.4)	(2.6)	(2.2)	(2.3)	(-0.1)	(-0.1)	(1.5)
ΔTRS	0.0	0.000	0.047	0.09	0.071	0.086	0.029	0.29	0.02
		(0.0)	(4.4)	(3.4)	(5.0)	(1.4)	(0.4)	(2.0)	(1.0)
ΔBTD	0.0	0.019	-0.008	-0.00	-0.022	-0.098	-0.033	-0.38	-0.02
		(1.4)	(-0.7)	(-0.0)	(-1.3)	(-1.3)	(-0.4)	(-2.1)	(-0.8)
ΔBSD	0.0	0.027	0.138	0.43	0.173	0.317	0.125	1.48	0.01
		(1.3)	(6.7)	(8.4)	(6.2)	(2.6)	(0.9)	(5.2)	(0.1)
ΔNATSAV	0.0	-0.007	0.006	0.00	-0.012	-0.035	0.034	0.33	0.01
		(-1.3)	(1.1)	(0.0)	(-1.7)	(-1.1)	(1.1)	(4.3)	(0.2)
ΔPSD	0.0	0.018	-0.018	0.00	-0.038	-0.159	0.439	-0.24	0.03
		(1.8)	(-1.7)	(0.0)	(-2.8)	(-2.7)	(6.9)	(-1.8)	(1.6)
ΔDWE	0.31	-0.093	0.857	0.44	0.816	0.133	0.456	1.06	0.00
	(7.3)	(-3.8)	(42.0)	(7.8)	(26.7)	(0.9)	(3.0)	(3.6)	(0.0)
ΔCD	0.0	0.012	0.028	0.05	0.043	0.662	0.097	-1.06	0.10
		(0.7)	(1.6)	(1.2)	(1.9)	(6.5)	(0.9)	(-4.4)	(3.5)
-ΔCONCR	0.0	0.012	-0.004	0.02	-0.007	0.063	-0.049	-0.27	-0.04
		(1.8)	(-0.6)	(1.6)	(-0.8)	(1.7)	(-1.2)	(-2.9)	(-3.0)
-ΔLHP	-0.31	0.026	-0.064	-0.06	-0.038	-0.038	-0.096	-1.20	-0.12
	*	*	*	*	*	*	*	*	*

Table 6A.6
Dynamic coefficients - restricted model

	-ΔPE	ΔRBTD	ΔRBSD	ΔRNATSAV	ΔRPSD	ΔRCONCR	ΔRLHP
ΔCON	0.0	0.0	0.0	0.0	0.0	0.01 (1.1)	0.0
ΔTRS	0.12 *	0.0	-0.04 (-0.5)	-0.08 (-1.8)	0.0	0.0	0.0
ΔBTD	0.0	0.18 *	-0.24 (-3.9)	0.06 (2.3)	0.0	0.0	0.0
ΔBSD	-0.04 (-0.5)	-0.24 (-3.9)	0.50 *	-0.16 (-4.4)	-0.06 (-1.5)	0.0	0.0
ΔNATSAV	-0.08 (-1.8)	0.06 (2.3)	-0.16 (-4.4)	0.21 *	0.03 (2.1)	0.0	0.0
ΔPSD	0.0	0.0	-0.06 (-1.5)	0.03 (2.1)	0.03 *	0.0	0.0
ΔDWE	0.0	0.0	0.0	0.0	0.0	0.0	-0.08 (-1.6)
ΔCD	0.0	0.0	0.0	0.0	0.0	-0.06 (-1.8)	0.0
-ΔCONCR	0.0	0.0	0.0	0.0	0.0	0.05 (1.2)	0.0
-ΔLHP	0.0	0.0	0.0	0.0	0.0	0.0	0.08 (2.3)

	ΔLVR	ΔEQ	ΔNW$_{-1}$	ΔY	ΔCGDWE	ΔCGCD	ΔCGPSD	D	T
ΔCON	0.0	-0.015	0.015	0.03	0.014	0.088	-0.016	0.01	0.02
		(-3.2)	(3.1)	(2.7)	(2.3)	(3.2)	(-0.6)	(0.1)	(2.4)
ΔTRS	0.0	0.00	0.046	0.09	0.074	0.113	0.019	0.35	0.01
		(0.0)	(4.3)	(4.1)	(5.1)	(1.8)	(0.3)	(2.3)	(0.8)
ΔBTD	0.0	0.015	-0.001	0.05	-0.004	-0.023	-0.000	-0.25	-0.03
		(1.2)	(-0.1)	(1.8)	(-0.3)	(-0.3)	(-0.0)	(-1.4)	(-1.3)
ΔBSD	0.0	0.041	0.154	0.41	0.158	0.166	0.221	1.18	-0.02
		(2.0)	(7.6)	(8.5)	(5.8)	(1.4)	(1.8)	(4.3)	(-0.8)
ΔNATSAV	0.0	-0.009	0.003	0.00	-0.012	-0.021	0.020	0.36	0.01
		(-1.5)	(0.6)	(0.0)	(-1.6)	(-0.7)	(0.6)	(4.5)	(0.6)
ΔPSD	0.0	0.012	-0.036	-0.03	-0.044	-0.139	0.347	-0.18	0.06
		(1.1)	(-3.3)	(-1.4)	(-3.2)	(-2.3)	(5.4)	(-1.2)	(3.2)
ΔDWE	0.31	-0.093	0.856	0.44	0.815	0.128	0.458	1.06	0.0
	(7.2)	(-3.8)	(42.0)	(7.8)	(26.7)	(0.9)	(3.1)	(3.6)	
ΔCD	0.0	0.010	0.029	0.05	0.046	0.671	0.097	-1.04	0.10
		(0.6)	(1.6)	(1.3)	(0.5)	(6.5)	(0.9)	(-4.2)	(3.5)
-ΔCONCR	0.0	0.012	-0.003	0.02	-0.006	0.062	-0.046	-0.27	-0.04
		(1.8)	(-0.5)	(1.6)	(-0.7)	(1.7)	(-1.2)	(-2.9)	(-3.0)
-ΔLHP	-0.31	0.027	-0.063	-0.06	-0.041	-0.045	-0.100	-1.22	-0.11
	*	*	*	*	*	*	*	*	*

Table 6A.8
Adjustment coefficients

	CON	TRS	BTD	BSD	NATSAV	PSD	DWE	CD	CONCR
ΔCON	-0.91	0.17	0.17	0.09	0.15	0.05	0.06	0.16	0.0
	(-6.1)	(2.6)	(3.1)	(3.0)	(1.3)	(1.0)	(1.3)	(3.3)	
ΔTRS	0.08	-0.50	-0.03	-0.04	0.0	0.02	0.02	0.04	0.45
	(0.3)	(-3.6)	(-0.3)	(-0.5)		(0.3)	(0.3)	(0.4)	(2.5)
ΔBTD	0.0	-0.09	-0.35	0.15	0.0	-0.24	0.16	0.18	0.12
		(-0.7)	(-2.5)	(2.3)		(-2.2)	(2.4)	(2.5)	(0.9)
ΔBSD	0.0	0.0	0.07	-0.43	0.0	-0.13	0.16	0.08	0.0
			(0.3)	(-4.9)		(-0.7)	(1.4)	(0.6)	
ΔNATSAV	-0.17	0.35	-0.08	0.13	-0.71	0.35	0.15	0.07	-0.09
	(-1.3)	(3.9)	(-1.2)	(3.4)	(-5.7)	(5.4)	(3.5)	(1.5)	(-0.9)
ΔPSD	-0.40	-0.08	-0.15	0.24	0.0	-0.38	0.27	0.27	0.23
	(-1.6)	(-0.6)	(-1.1)	(3.5)		(-3.8)	(4.4)	(3.2)	(3.7)
ΔDWE	0.0	0.0	1.17	-0.14	1.08	-0.05	-0.92	-0.32	-0.14
			(4.1)	(-1.2)	(4.0)	(-0.2)	(-5.8)	(-2.1)	(-0.7)
ΔCD	1.03	-0.10	-0.48	-0.06	0.0	0.05	-0.08	-0.37	0.0
	(2.8)	(-0.6)	(-2.5)	(-0.5)		(0.3)	(-0.8)	(-2.8)	
-ΔCONCR	-0.12	0.19	0.11	0.05	0.0	0.09	0.02	-0.06	-0.56
	(-0.6)	(1.9)	(1.4)	(1.0)		(1.3)	(0.3)	(-1.0)	(-5.1)
-ΔLHP	0.49	0.06	-0.43	0.01	-0.52	0.24	0.16	-0.05	-0.01
	*	*	*	*	*	*	*	*	*

Table 6A.9
Diagnostic statistics

	R^2	B-P(8)
ΔCON	0.99	19.7
ΔTRS	0.73	13.0
ΔBTD	0.63	20.8
ΔBSD	0.81	9.0
ΔNATSAV	0.63	5.7
ΔPSD	0.82	13.6
ΔDWE	0.98	1.7
ΔCD	0.71	9.7
-ΔCONCR	0.58	15.4
-ΔLHP	0.88	7.0

NB. The Box-Pierce B-P(k) statistic is a statistic for testing serial correlation of order 1 to k. Under the null hypothesis of no serial correlation it is asymptotically distributed as central chi-squared with k degrees of freedom. Critical values are :

5% significance level	15.5
1% - -	20.1

Table 6A.10

Model tracking performance

Static simulation: Actual exogenous variables

(1976:02 to 1987:04)

	RMSE	MAS	ME	U
CON	184.0	145.3	0.31	0.09
TRS	400.2	322.5	-0.23	0.49
BTD	483.6	360.4	0.10	0.61
BSD	838.9	639.8	-1.88	0.39
NATSAV	239.1	186.7	-104.60	0.57
PSD	408.4	321.4	0.65	0.42
DWE	1111.7	910.7	-3.2	0.11
CD	1327.1	1035.7	6.0	0.79
-CONCR	272.4	214.5	-0.71	0.40
-LHP	523.5	373.6	103.60	0.24

NB. RMSE = root mean square error

MAS = mean absolute error

ME   = mean error

U   = Theil's inequality coefficient

Appendix 6B
Tracking performance

This appendix contains plots of in-sample tracking exercises.

The figure 6A series are the static tracks and show actual against predicted values for the dependent variables with the predicted values obtained by cumulatively adding the predicted changes to the 1976 Q1 starting values.

The figure 6B series show dynamic tracks where predicted values of lagged variables are used.

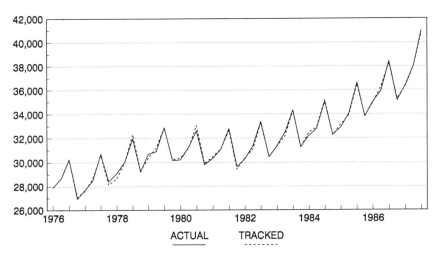

Figure 6A.1 Static Track: Consumption

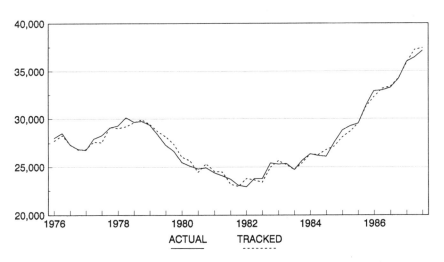

Figure 6A.2 Static Track: Transaction Stocks

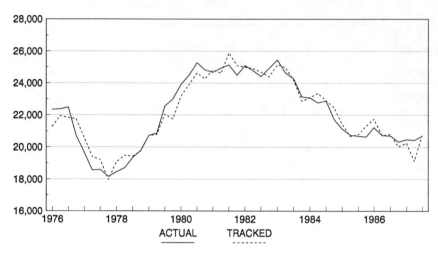

Figure 6A.3 Static Track: Bank Time Deposits

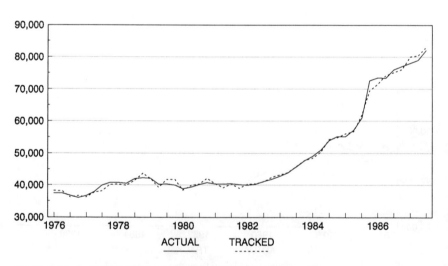

Figure 6A.4 Static Track: Building Society Deposits

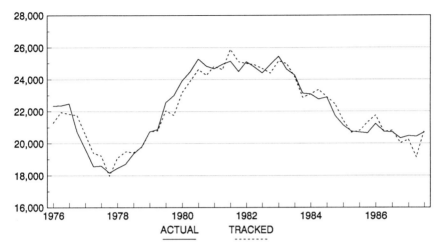

Figure 6A.3 Static Track: Bank Time Deposits

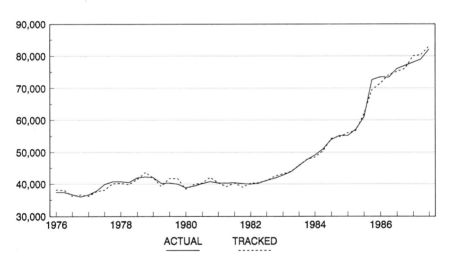

Figure 6A.4 Static Track: Building Society Deposits

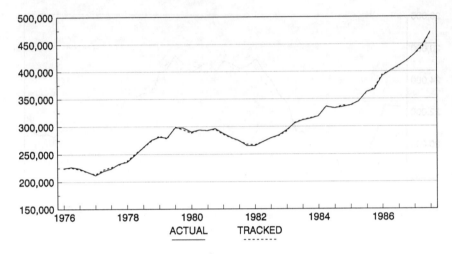

Figure 6A.7 Static Track: Dwellings

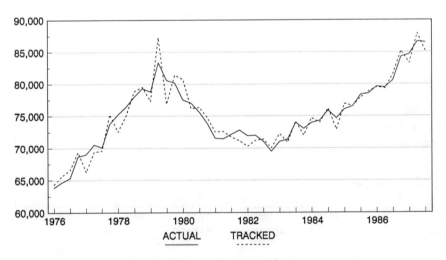

Figure 6A.8 Static Track: Consumer Durables

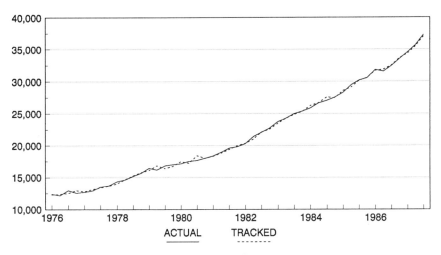

Figure 6A.9 Static Track: Consumer Credit

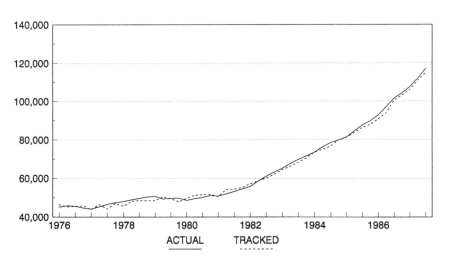

Figure 6A.10 Static Track: Loans for House Purchase

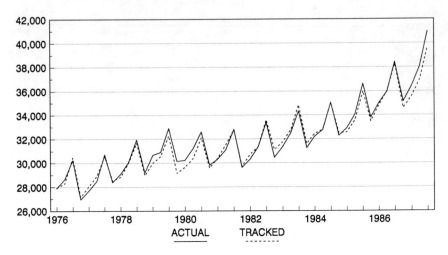

Figure 6B.1 Dynamic Track: Consumption

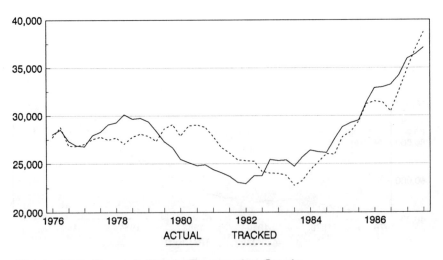

Figure 6B.2 Dynamic Track: Transaction Stocks

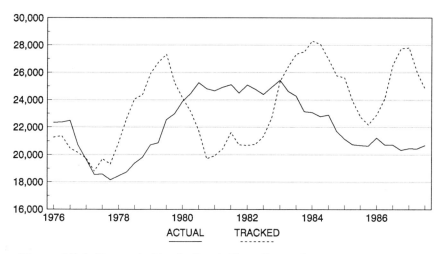

Figure 6B.3 Dynamic Track: Bank Time Deposits

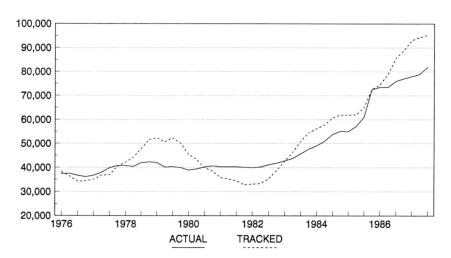

Figure 6B.4 Dynamic Track: Building Society Deposits

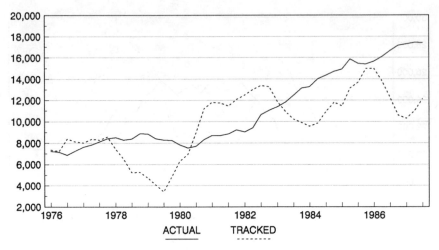

Figure 6B.5 Dynamic Track: National Savings

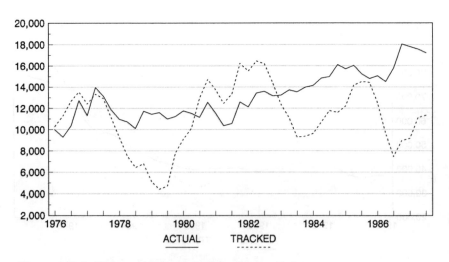

Figure 6B.6 Dynamic Track: Public Sector Debt

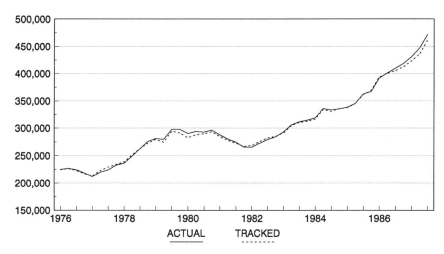

Figure 6B.7 Dynamic Track: Dwellings

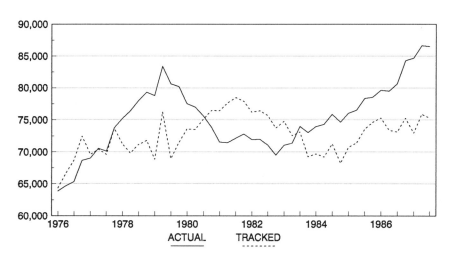

Figure 6B.8 Dynamic Track: Consumer Durables

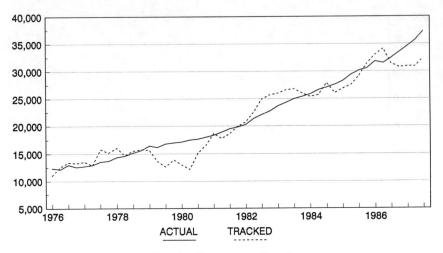

Figure 6B.9 Dynamic Track: Consumer Credit

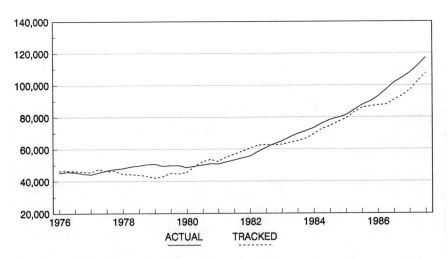

Figure 6B.10 Dynamic Track: Loans for House Purchase

7 Simulation experiments

7.1 Introduction

The preferred model described in the last chapter was used to conduct several simulation experiments. The results of these simulations provide useful insights into some policy issues. One issue which has been the subject of much debate recently concerns the most appropriate method of controlling the expansion of credit. However, whilst a good deal of discussion has taken place on this issue there have been few empirical studies conducted in this area. The model developed in this study provides a useful framework to examine alternative policies designed to control credit. Other related issues to the control of credit are also considered in the simulation experiments reported in this chapter. The first experiment examines another possible explanation for the growth of credit that has occurred over the 1980's, which is the reduction in spread between lending and borrowing rates. A second experiment examines the effects of greater expected capital gain on housing and provides an insight into how real and financial decision making has become more inter-related over the 1980's.

A secondary feature of the simulation studies reported in this chapter is that they provide a further opportunity to examine the plausibility of the model. In judging the plausibility of the simulation results reference will be made to economic theory and observations of Personal Sector behaviour described in earlier chapters of this study.

The plan of this chapter is as follows. In section 7.2 the method of simulation is briefly described followed in section 7.3 by a discussion of the base runs from the simulation experiments. The main simulation experiments carried out examined the issue of controlling credit. To this end the effects of imposing direct controls on credit were compared with the effects of raising interest rates and the results of these experiments are reported in section 7.4. Additional simulation experiments examined the effects of a reduced spread between lending and borrowing rates and greater expected capital gains and the results of these are reported in section 7.5.

7.2 Method of simulation

The model was simulated by fixing all the exogenous variables at their 1976 quarter one values and then allowing the system to run to convergence. The resulting profiles formed the base runs. A simulation experiment was then conducted by changing a chosen exogenous variable after the system has run for eight quarters (in 1978, quarter 2). The changed exogenous variable produces new desired values for the endogenous variables and the system adjusts to the new equilibrium through the error-correction dynamic equations.

It is important to consider again the nature of the model used to conduct the simulation experiments before we examine any results. The model developed in this research is an allocation model whereby some pre-determined sum (existing wealth + income + capital gains) is allocated across consumption, financial assets, real assets and liabilities. The model is therefore only a partial model of Personal Sector behaviour and the main policy instruments in the model are interest rates. To illustrate the limitations of using a such a partial model for simulation experiments it is helpful to consider the channels through which interest rates affect an economy. The most direct effect of a rise in interest rates is to make saving more attractive and borrowing more expensive (and hence reduce planned investment). A second direct effect operates through disposable income which partly consists of interest payments net of receipts. Second round income effects will also occur as the direct effects influence the level of economic activity. A third effect of interest rate increases is to reduce the value of assets such as equities, housing and government bonds. The reduction in wealth that occurs is likely to reduce expenditure. A final interest rate channel that can be discerned operates through the exchange rate. A rise in domestic interest rates relative to foreign rates is likely to lead to an exchange rate appreciation. This is likely to lead to a reduction in import prices in the domestic economy and a rise in export prices in foreign economies both of which are likely to reduce aggregate demand and hence put downward pressure on inflation. The preceding discussion illustrates the variety of channels through which changes in interest rates can affect economic activity. The model developed in this study only captures the first of these effects ie. the direct portfolio effects on borrowing and lending and hence abstracts from any further portfolio changes caused by changes to income induced trough the other channels.

Before considering the results of the simulation experiments it also needs to be noted that model is open to the 'Lucas' critique. Lucas (1976) pointed out that unless the estimated equations of the model used to conduct simulation experiments are genuinely structural or behavioural then any results from such simulations may be seriously flawed. This is because when expectations are formed rationally then agents react to the behaviour of government. Thus the parameters of any non-structural equations will implicitly depend on the government policy rule in operation and when alternative policy rules are simulated the parameters are also likely to be different.

7.3 Base runs

Plots of the base runs for the experiments are presented in figures 7A.1 to 7A.10 in appendix 7. The first point to note about these is the non-monotonic nature of the adjustment paths. The two main divergers from monotonic adjustment paths are bank time deposits and public sector debt. It is quite likely that there is a problem in the adjustment specification of one of these assets which is then passed to others because of the complementary nature of the adjustment of these assets as evidenced by their adjustment coefficients. The next most divergent from monotonic adjustment is transaction stocks. This is quite likely reflecting the facilitating role of this asset as households adjust to their equilibrium position. The other adjustments do not diverge too seriously from that of monotonic adjustment. It is difficult to comment on whether monotonic adjustment of assets to equilibrium is a desired property as economic theory is sparse in relation to the behaviour of households out of equilibrium. It is useful to note though that in two similar studies of personal sector portfolio behaviour, namely Hood (1987) and Barr and Cuthbertson (1989), that non-monotonic adjustment for some categories of liquid assets modelled was also found.

The plots of the base runs also show that the time taken for each asset to reach equilibrium is quite slow. The times taken (in years) in each case to reach equilibrium is summarised in the table below.

Table 7.1
Time taken to reach equilibrium

	90% adjustment	100% adjustment
Consumption	3	7
Transaction Stock	7	10
Bank time deposits	5	8
Building Soc. deposits	3	6
National Savings	4	10
Public Sector debt	5	10
Dwellings	3	10
Consumer durables	5	8
Consumer credit	7	11
Loans for house purchase	4	11

The times to achieve complete adjustment appear to be overly long, particularly for the short term financial assets and consumption where adjustment costs are low. However ninety per cent of the adjustment to the new equilibrium is achieved in most cases in a significantly shorter time. For transaction assets and consumer credit where 90% adjustment still takes a long time to achieve then this probably reflects again the nature of these instruments as facilitators of adjustment for the other instruments. The generally long adjustment times for financial assets found in this study may reflect habit persistence and the costs of obtaining information. Hood (1987) also finds slow speeds of adjustment in his study of personal sector liquid asset demands (greater than 10 years for some).

7.4 Controlling credit

In this section we report the results of three simulation experiments which explore the effects of different ways of controlling credit. The first two experiments examine direct controls, firstly in the loans for house purchase market and secondly on total bank lending. The third experiment examines the alternative policy of raising interest rates. In the final part of this section, in the light of the simulation results, some of the problems of controlling credit will be discussed.

7.4.1 Decrease the loan to value ratio (LVR)

The LVR ratio is used in this model as a proxy for rationing in the loans for house purchase market. By lowering the ratio house loan rationing increases.

In the base run the LVR ratio is set at its 1976 quarter one value which is 0.787. In the simulation run the LVR ratio is lowered by 0.05 to 0.737 which is close to the value of LVR when rationing in the mortgage market was tight in the period 1978 to 1981. This level of LVR means that the amount borrowed cannot exceed 73.7% (compared with 78.7% before the change) of the value of the house on average. Another way of stating this is to say that on average, the borrower must provide from their own resources 37.3% (32.3%) of the purchase price of the house.

It needs to be noted that the LVR variable only appears in the two equations where it has a direct effect, namely dwellings and loans for house purchase. Thus a change in LVR will only affect demand for dwellings and loans for house purchase in the long run. The effects on the other demands will only be temporary as the model moves to a new equilibrium. Plots of the simulation run and base are provided in figures 7B.1 to 7B.10 in appendix 7. The effects on dwellings and loans for house purchase are immediate with approximately 95% of the downward adjustment taking place in the first quarter. The final reduction in loans for house purchase and hence the value of housing is approximately £2000m. Such rapid effect is to be expected as this is a direct control which would be difficult to evade. As loans for house purchase have been leaking into the purchase of financial assets over a large part of the estimation period of the model (discussed in chapter six, page 115) then a temporary reduction in bank time deposits and building society deposits following a reduction in loans for house purchase is plausible. The increase in longer term financial assets as short term assets decline is also plausible reflecting the substitutability of longer and short term assets. Consumer credit rises in the short run possibly reflecting substitutability with loans for house purchase. The rise in consumer credit also appears to lead to a short term rise in consumption and consumer durables demand.

The conclusions of this simulation experiment are that the model produces results which appear reasonable and that a return to a lower loan to value ratio would have an immediate reducing effect on loans for house purchase. The substitutability between loans for house purchase and consumer credit suggests that restrictions on loans for house purchase would be more effective if backed by similar restrictions on consumer credit. The implications of these conclusions are discussed in section 7.4.4 below.

7.4.2 Re-introduction of direct controls on bank lending

In the model an on-off dummy variable was used as a crude proxy for the effects of direct controls on bank lending. The dummy is set to zero when controls are in operation and one otherwise. A new base run was obtained with all exogenous variables set to their 1976 quarter one values as before, but in addition the dummy representing bank controls set to one. In the simulation experiment the dummy was changed to zero in 1978, quarter two. The effects of this can be seen in the plots presented in figures 7C.1 to 7C.10 in appendix 7 which in particular show a fall in total credit (ie. consumer credit and loans for house purchase) of approximately £14500m. The move to a new equilibrium takes longer when compared to the other direct control instrument considered in the last section. This is because the control on bank lending dummy appears in each equation (unlike LVR) and so there will be more interaction between adjustment paths. The move to the new equilibrium in the consumer credit equation is particularly slow, which is surprising as the aim of

165

introducing controls is to directly affect this variable. The most immediate effect though is to reduce consumption which in fact goes on to overshoot the new equilibrium before settling down. Stocks of transaction money increase after the introduction of lending controls probably reflecting a switch from credit to cash to manage spending needs. All the other financial asset stocks reduce after the introduction of controls which is a plausible result reflecting households running down liquid asset stocks in order to maintain planned consumption levels (this hypothesis was put forward to explain the decline in liquid asset stocks in the 1970's when restrictions on credit were in place - see for example, Bank of England (1987)). Loans for house purchase also reduce slowly after the introduction of controls and this reduction is reflected in a reduction in stocks of dwellings. A counter-intuitive result is the increase in consumer durable stocks albeit after an initial fall. This appears to be financed by the run down of liquid assets. This odd result for consumer durables can be traced back to the 'wrong' sign, on a priori grounds, on the bank lending controls dummy in the long run equation for consumer durables and this suggests that this equation needs further attention in any future development of the model. In addition whilst the results just discussed are broadly reasonable they perhaps do not capture the true effects of the introduction of lending controls as the dummy variable used to represent this is only a crude proxy. Further work therefore also needs to be done to find a more representative variable to capture the effects of controls.

7.4.3 Increase all interest rates by 4%

In order to further judge the effectiveness of direct controls on lending, discussed in the previous two sections, an alternative policy to reduce lending, that of increasing the cost of borrowing by raising interest rates, will now be considered. Rather than simply increasing interest rates on lending, a more realistic experiment would be to increase all interest rates in the model by the same amount. The base and simulation run for this experiment are shown in figures 7D.1 to 7D.10 in appendix 7 from which it can be discerned that total credit falls by approximately £1200m.

The first point to note is that it was only by raising interest rates by a large amount ie. 4% or more that significant effects on spending and credit could be found. The effectiveness of raising interest rates to control credit can be seen in the plot for loans for house purchase where it takes about four years to achieve 90% of the reducing effect of the higher interest rates. In addition the reducing effect builds up slowly over these four years. A reduction in consumer credit takes even longer to achieve than loans for house purchase. In addition the initial effect (after the first two quarters) of raising interest rates is to boost consumer credit. This is possibly explained by a reduction in holdings of transaction balances, because of a greater opportunity cost in holding such balances at higher real rates of interest, bringing consumer credit into play to facilitate adjustment. Another feature of these results is the weak effect of interest rates on consumer credit. The effect of higher interest rates though is to reduce consumption and to do so quickly. The effect of higher interest rates on consumer credit though appears to be very small and minimal in the long run.

7.4.4 Policies for controlling credit

In this section we examine the efficacy of credit controls as opposed to interest rate policy. At this stage an important caveat to this discussion needs to be mentioned. The model used for these simulations describes only household portfolio behaviour and therefore as noted at the outset to section 7.2, excludes many of the channels by which interest rates affect aggregate demand. Consequently the following analysis applies to the control of the proximate target of credit rather than the more distant target of aggregate demand and the ultimate targets of inflation and employment.

Credit controls were a weapon in the armoury of the

authorities up until 1980. The growth in credit over the 1980's has prompted discussion as to whether the abandonment of this weapon and the almost total reliance on interest rates to control credit was a wise decision. It has been argued by some commentators that the rapid growth of credit after the removal of restrictions in 1980 was due to households re-adjusting their portfolios. The rapid growth immediately after the removal of controls did appear to represent a release of pent up demand. However the growth in credit has continued beyond any plausible period of re-adjustment. An alternative explanation for the growth in credit, that is financial innovation, is discussed in section 7.5 below.

The current policy of using interest rates to control credit expansion has been criticised as being too slow to take effect and in having undesirable side effects, in particular the effect of reducing planned investment. Credit controls it is argued are a more precise weapon in that they act quickly and directly upon credit growth. However there are a number of problems associated with credit controls which will now be considered. The experience of credit controls in the 1970's showed that they have the effect of building up a demand for credit which explodes when the controls are released. This would suggest that temporary controls are not effective as they simply put off the problem of credit expansion to a later date and possibly even make the later problem worse. The structure of the markets for household credit have changed since the 1970's making it much more difficult to place controls on the balance sheets of the lending institutions which was the method in the 1970's. The banks increasingly place business off the balance sheet and therefore would not need to place restrictions on their loan customers if ceilings were placed on their assets or liabilities. Quantity constraints would be more effective on building societies which currently do not pursue "off-balance" sheet business. However to single out building societies would be seen as discriminatory and may lead the societies to innovate to escape controls. An example of one such innovation would be to securitise part of their mortgage assets so they could be sold on. Such innovations are more likely in the current internationally competitive financial environment. One type of credit control which escapes these criticisms, suggested by Sheilds (1988) is to apply the controls to the borrower rather than the lender. This could be applied by either introducing terms controls, such as the deposit/repayment terms which used to apply to hire purchase, or taxing credit. If this discussion is restricted to terms controls as this is more relevant to the simulations carried out then as mortgage lending is the most dominant form of both new and outstanding debt of households, terms control applied to mortgage lending would appear to be the most effective method of controlling credit. This could easily be achieved by the authorities setting an appropriate loan to purchase price ratio (ie. LVR ratio). This policy would of course have distorting effects in that it is left to the judgement of the authorities as to where to set the ratio and if and when it should be changed. This would go against the liberalisation philosophy in relation to financial markets which has existed since 1980. The policy would also hit first time buyers the hardest as it would force them to find larger deposits to finance the buying of the house than at present. However the problems of using direct credit controls would need to be judged against the problems of using interest rates only.

The preceding discussion finds support for a Loan to Value (LVR) type of credit control as an alternative to the sole use of interest rates. Support for the re-introduction of a lower loan to value (LVR) ratio to control credit is also found in the simulation experiments discussed above. It is apparent that lowering the LVR has an immediate reducing effect on credit. The results also suggested that controlling only one part of credit will be be negated in its effects by households switching to alternative forms of credit. The opportunities for such switching will clearly be limited but can be dealt with by introducing controls on alternative forms of credit to loans for house purchase. Introducing quantity controls also appears to achieve the same result albeit at a slower pace than the introduction of a lower LVR. However this, it was argued above, may be due to the construction of the model and therefore needs further investigation. The raising of interest rates again had the desired effect of lowering credit, however this took a long period of time to achieve and in addition the effects were weak requiring large rises in interest rates to achieve a significant reduction in credit. The weak effects of interest rates on borrowing and expenditure is evidenced by the small elasticities found in this study (see chapter 6, page 116). There is also supporting evidence for the slowness of the effect of raised interest rates to be transmitted through to reduced expenditure from the recent experience of the authorities attempts to reduce expenditure and inflation by raising interest rates.

7.5 Additional simulations

Additional simulation experiments were conducted to enable an examination of two related issues of Personal Sector behaviour over the 1980's. The first experiment examines the effects of one aspect of financial innovation, namely a reduction in the spread between borrowing and lending rates. This provides a possible further explanation of the growth in lending, to that of the easing of restrictions on lending. The second experiment examines one of the consequences of credit growth. It has been suggested (see Bank of England (1989)) that one consequence of the greater availability of credit has been to push up house prices. Over the period 1980 to 1988 house prices rose by 100% whilst retail prices increased by approximately 60%. This increase in house prices resulted in large capital gains for most house owners which together with a greater availability of credit (in particular second mortgages and other advances secured on the property but not used for housing improvements) has enabled owners to withdraw cash from the housing stock. This in turn has financed expenditure and financial asset acquisition (the latter despite a fall in the saving ratio). Another way in which greater capital gains on housing may have influenced expenditure and financial decisions is through a wealth effect. That is, as capital gains make house owners feel more wealthy they may reduce saving and hence increase consumption. From this discussion it can be seen that the real decision about house purchase is very much related to other real and financial decisions. Therefore the second simulation experiment which examines the effects of increased expected capital gain on housing provides an opportunity to investigate an increasingly important aspect of the inter-related nature of household real and financial decisions.

7.5.1 Decrease rates of interest on borrowing by 1%

The effect of reducing only the rates of interest on borrowing is to reduce the spread between lending and borrowing rates for households. Such a reduction is argued to have occurred over the 1980's following liberalisation of financial markets and greater competition (see for example Rose (1986)). The results of this experiment are reported in figures 7E.1 to 7E.10 in appendix 7. The effects of the reduction in the spread on financial assets are seen to be temporary but whilst there is an effect this is to increase short term financial assets (transaction stocks, bank time deposits and building society deposits) and reduce longer term financial assets (national savings and public sector debt). An explanation for this may be that when it becomes less costly to borrow funds then there is less use made of short term assets to meet expenditure needs. It has been suggested (see Bank of England (1987) that over the 1970's the Personal sector ran down financial assets to maintain expenditure at desired levels but when borrowing became easier in the 1980's short term financial assets have risen to higher equilibrium levels. This appears to be reflected in this simulation experiment. The rise in short term financial assets, as mentioned above, appears to be at the expense of longer term financial assets. The effect of a reduction in spreads is clearly to increase borrowing in all its forms in the long run with the total increase being of the order of £600m. In the short run consumer credit increases and reduces probably reflecting its facilitating role as the system moves to a new equilibrium. Expenditure on dwellings, consumption and consumer durables all increase financed by the additional borrowed funds. These results are all generally acceptable and as outlined above provide an additional explanation for the growth of credit and the consequent growth of expenditure.

7.5.2 Increase expected capital gain on dwellings by £10bn

The results for this experiment are shown in figures 7F.1 to 7F.10 in appendix 7. An increase in expected capital gain on dwellings appears to initially boost short term financial assets (bank time deposits, building society deposits and transaction stocks) and depress longer term assets such as national savings and public sector debt. The rise in short term assets falls off in the long run and for bank time deposits the long run change is negative. Longer term assets gain moderately in the long run. Consumption after a slight fall initially shows a steady rise. Stocks of dwellings initially fall although end up gaining in the long run. The adjustment path of consumer durables is the strangest showing an initial rise then a fall before moving to a long run position of gain. The adjustment path for the two liabilities broadly reflect the adjustment for the longer term assets with an initial fall and then a rise in the long run. This set of adjustments appears to suggest that assets where the costs of adjustment are low seem to benefit immediately from the effect of a greater feeling of wealth as more capital gain is expected. This also follows for consumption where again costs of adjustment are low. For longer term assets where costs of adjustment are higher, particularly dwellings, then it takes a longer time for the adjustment to the long run position to occur. These adjustment paths are therefore broadly acceptable.

The results discussed in this section illustrate that one of the ways in which the liberalisation of credit markets has fed through to greater expenditure is through the release of equity from the housing market. A further conclusion that can be drawn from these results is that decisions about house purchase and wealth held as housing can be seen as part of the wider portfolio decision faced by households. This inter-relationship between and real and financial decisions is likely to have become greater over the 1980's.

7.6 Conclusion

The results of all the simulation experiments described above have provided some useful insights into some policy issues and trends in Personal sector behaviour over the 1980's that have been discussed in the literature. An investigation of alternative policies to control credit supported the use of a lower loan to value ratio in relation to loans for house purchase. Simulation experiments showed this instrument to act more quickly and effectively when compared with the alternative policies of introducing quantity controls on bank lending and raising interest rates. Whilst such an instrument would have drawbacks in any practical application it is thought that its precision and effectiveness in terms of difficulty of avoidance may make it a more desirable policy instrument than the other two described. The slow adjustment to interest rate changes indicated in section 7.4.3 substantiate the view that a fairly long period of high interest rates is necessary to damp down credit growth. An examination of the effects of a reduction in the spread between borrowing and lending rates appears to provide a further explanation, to that of the removal of restrictions on credit markets, for the rapid growth of credit that has occurred over the 1980's. Finally an investigation of another phenomenon of the 1980's, that of rapid growth of capital gains on dwellings illustrates one of the channels through which the liberalisation of credit markets led to the expenditure boom. The results also provide additional support for the underlying hypothesis of this research which is that real and financial decisions are inter-related.

The results obtained in all these simulation experiments are generally plausible, reflecting observed behaviour of the Personal sector, and therefore provide further support for the model developed in this study.

Appendix 7A
Simulation results

This appendix contains plots of the simulation experiments discussed in chapter 7. The series 7A presents the base runs for the simulations. Series 7B to 7F present the results of the experiments.

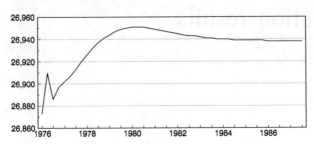

Figure 7A.1 Base Run: Consumption

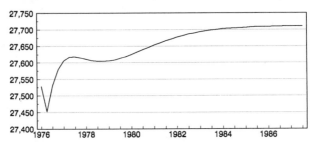

Figure 7A.2 Base Run: Transaction Stocks

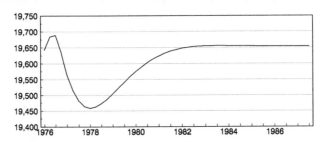

Figure 7A.3 Base Run: Bank Time Deposits

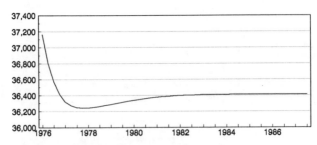

Figure 7A.4 Base Run: Building Society Deposits

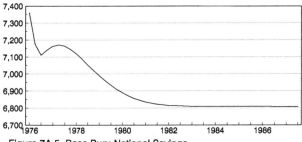
Figure 7A.5 Base Run: National Savings

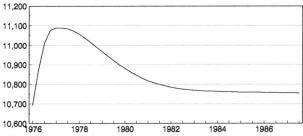
Figure 7A.6 Base Run: Public Sector Debt

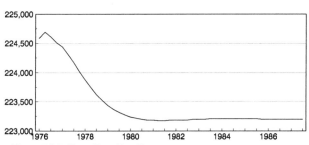
Figure 7A.7 Base Run: Dwellings

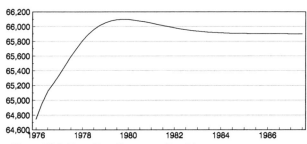
Figure 7A.8 Base Run: Consumer Durables

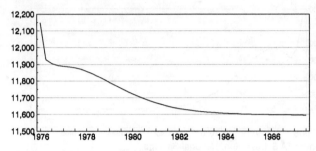

Figure 7A.9 Base Run: Consumer Credit

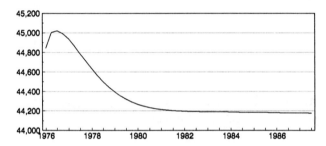

Figure 7A.10 Base Run: Loans for House Purchase

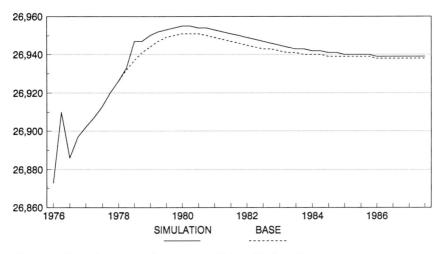

Figure 7B.1 Decrease in Loan to Value Ratio - Consumption

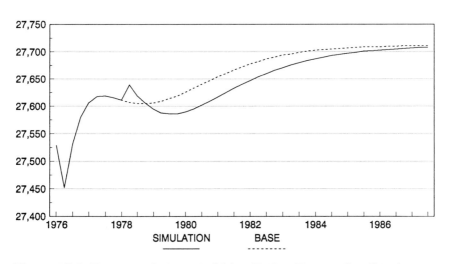

Figure 7B.2 Decrease in Loan to Value Ratio - Transaction Stocks

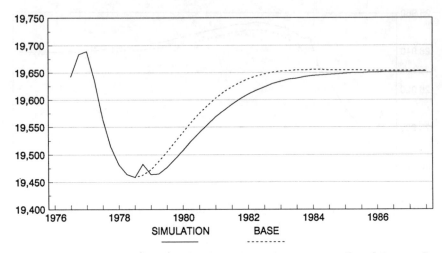

Figure 7B.3 Decrease in Loan to Value Ratio - Bank Time Deposits

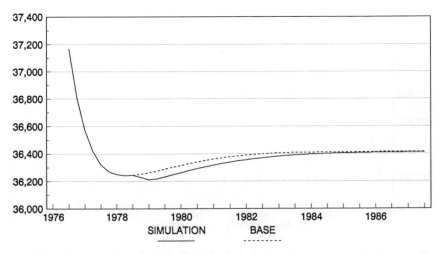

Figure 7B.4 Decrease in Loan to Value Ratio
- Building Society Deposits

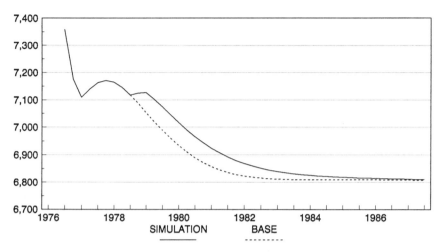

Figure 7B.5 Decrease in Loan to Value Ratio - National Savings

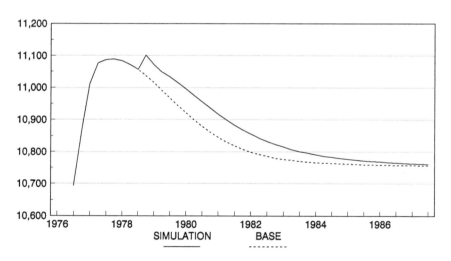

Figure 7B.6 Decrease in Loan to Value Ratio - Public Sector Debt

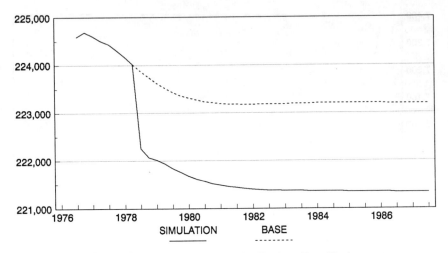

Figure 7B.7 Decrease in Loan to Value Ratio - Dwellings

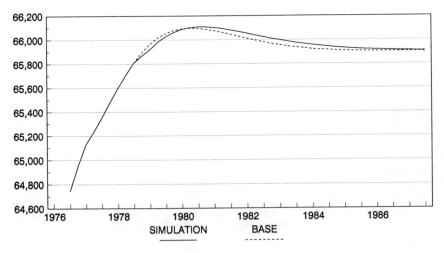

Figure 7B.8 Decrease in Loan to Value Ratio - Consumer Durables

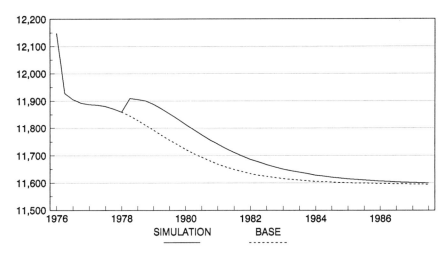

Figure 7B.9 Decrease in Loan to Value Ratio - Consumer Credit

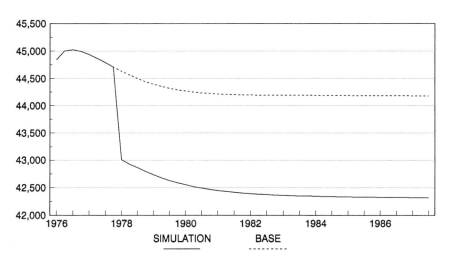

Figure 7B.10 Decrease in Loan to Value Ratio
- Loans for House Purchase

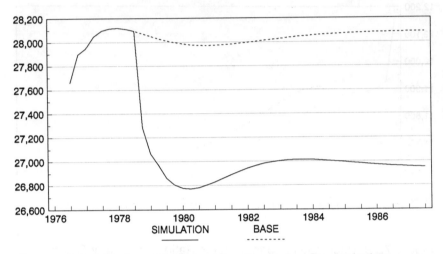

Figure 7C.1 Introduce Direct Lending Controls - Consumption

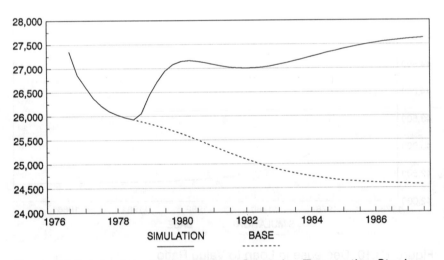

Figure 7C.2 Introduce Direct Lending Controls - Transaction Stocks

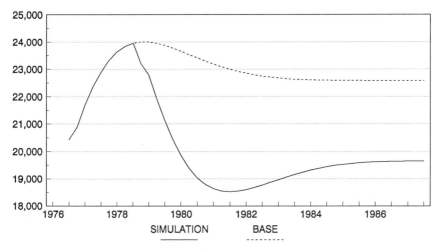

Figure 7C.3 Introduce Direct Lending Controls
- Bank Time Deposits

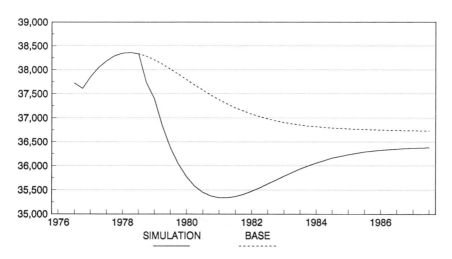

Figure 7C.4 Introduce Direct Lending Controls
- Building Society Deposits

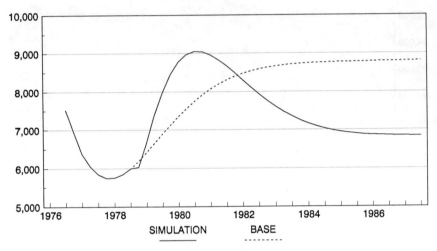

Figure 7C.5 Introduce Direct Lending Controls
- National Savings

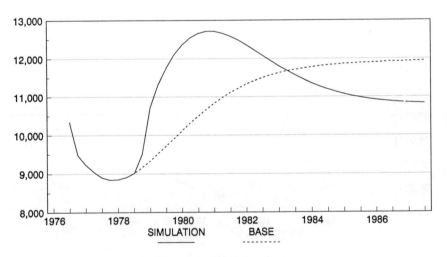

Figure 7C.6 Introduce Direct Lending Controls
- Public Sector Debt

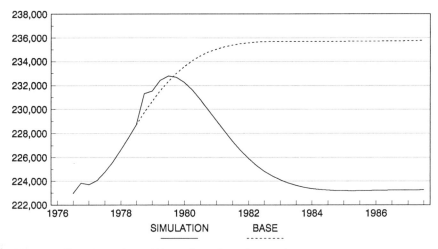

Figure 7C.7 Introduce Direct Lending Controls
              - Dwellings

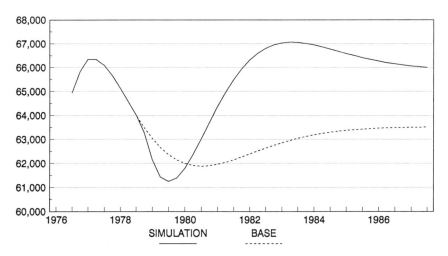

Figure 7C.8 Introduce Direct Lending Controls
              - Consumer Durables

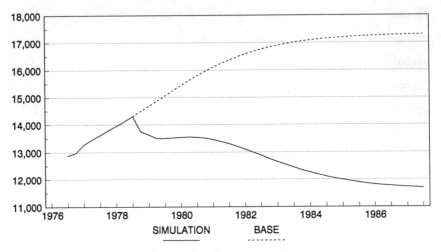

Figure 7C.9 Introduce Direct Lending Controls
- Consumer Credit

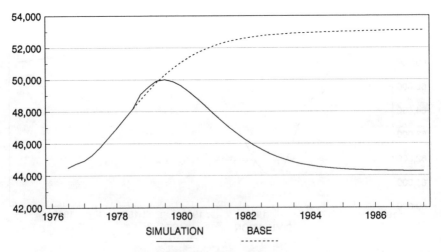

Figure 7C.10 Introduce Direct Lending Controls
- Loans for House Purchase

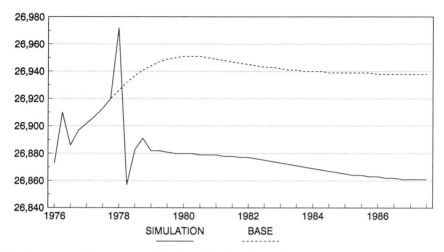

Figure 7D.1 Increase all Interest Rates by 4%
- Consumption

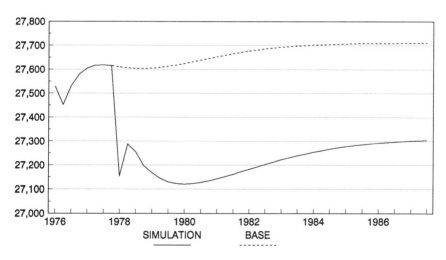

Figure 7D.2 Increase all Interest Rates by 4%
- Transaction Stocks

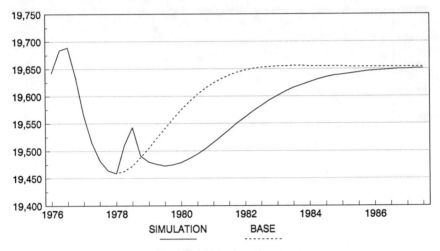

Figure 7D.3 Increase all Interest Rates by 4%
- Bank Time Deposits

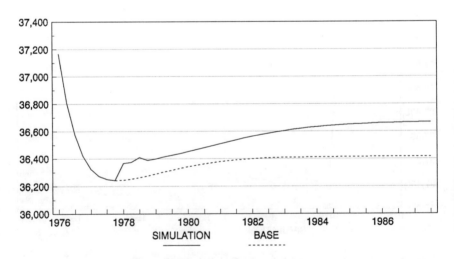

Figure 7D.4 Increase all Interest Rates by 4%
- Building Society Deposits

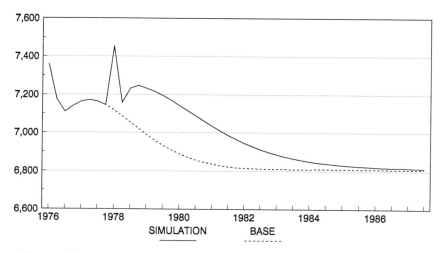

Figure 7D.5 Increase all Interest Rates by 4%
- National Savings

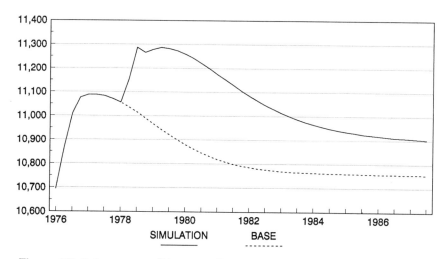

Figure 7D.6 Increase all Interest Rates by 4%
- Public Sector Debt

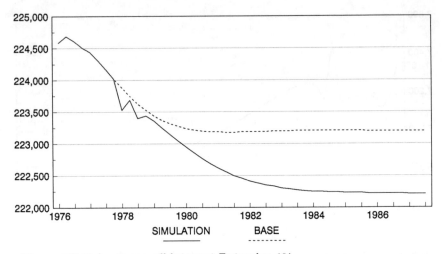

Figure 7D.7 Increase all Interest Rates by 4%
- Dwellings

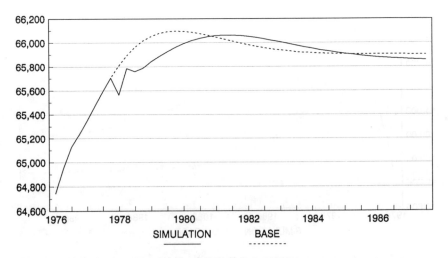

Figure 7D.8 Increase all Interest Rates by 4%
- Consumer Durables

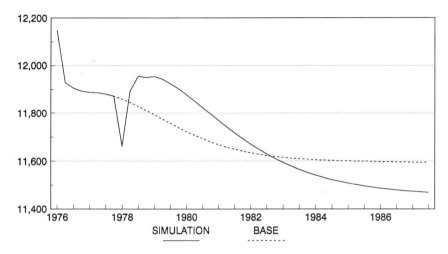

Figure 7D.9 Increase all Interest Rates by 4%
- Consumer Credit

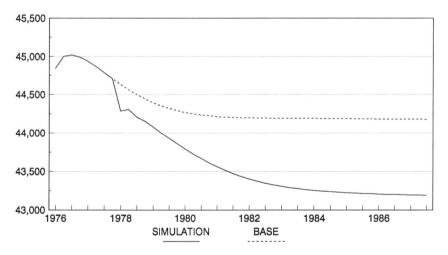

Figure 7D.10 Increase all Interest Rates by 4%
- Loans for House Purchase

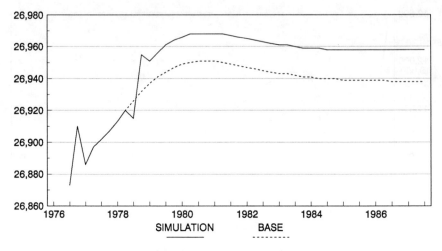

Figure 7E.1 Decrease Borrowing Rates by 1%
- Consumption

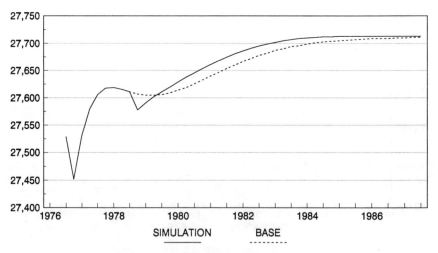

Figure 7E.2 Decrease borrowing rates by 1%
- Transaction Stocks

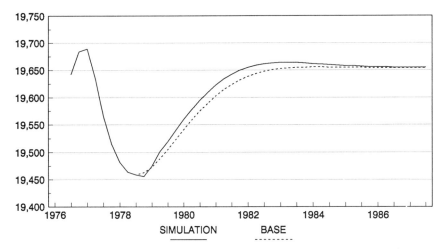

Figure 7E.3 Decrease Borrowing Rates by 1%
        - Bank Time Deposits

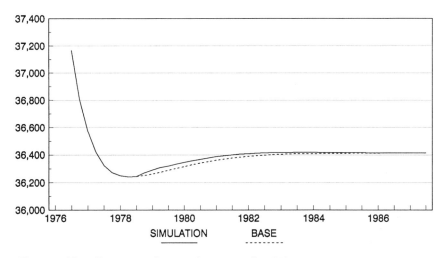

Figure 7E.4 Decrease borrowing rates by 1%
        - Building Society Deposits

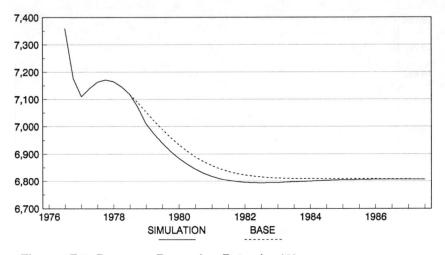

Figure 7E.5 Decrease Borrowing Rates by 1%
- National Savings

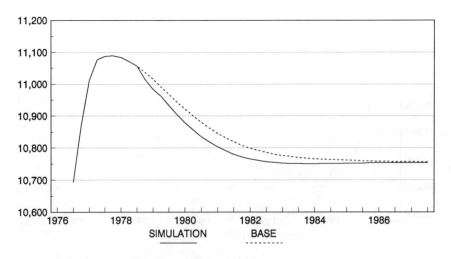

Figure 7E.6 Decrease borrowing rates by 1%
- Public Sector Debt

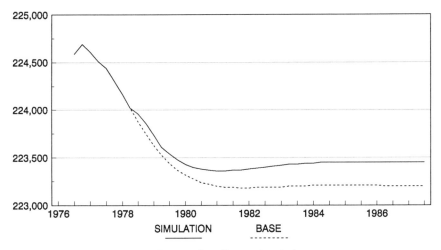

Figure 7E.7 Decrease Borrowing Rates by 1%
- Dwellings

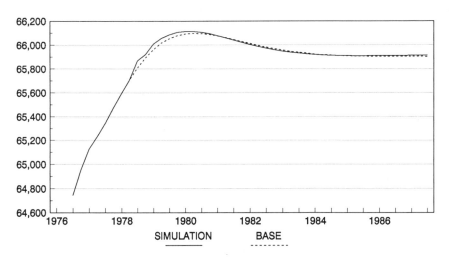

Figure 7E.8 Decrease borrowing rates by 1%
- Consumer Durables

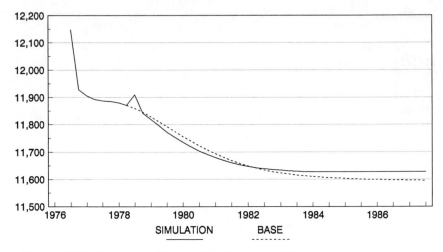

Figure 7E.9 Decrease Borrowing Rates by 1%
- Consumer Credit

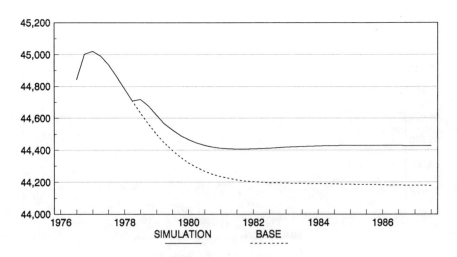

Figure 7E.10 Decrease borrowing rates by 1%
- Loans for House Purchase

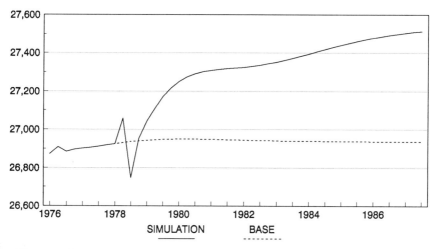

Figure 7F.1 Increase expected capital gain on dwellings by £10bn
- Consumption

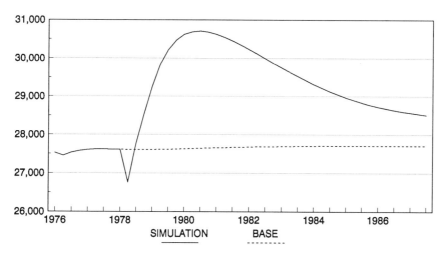

Figure 7F.2 Increase expected capital gain on dwellings by £10bn
- Transaction Stocks

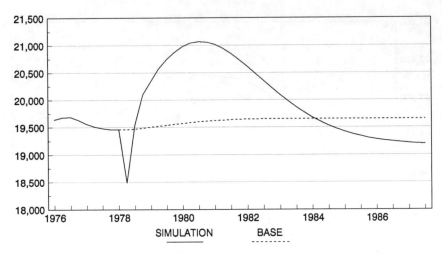

Figure 7F.3 Increase expected capital gain on dwellings by £10bn
- Bank Time Deposits

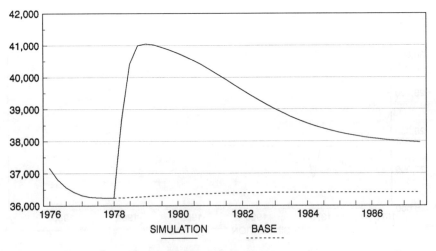

Figure 7F.4 Increase expected capital gain on dwellings by £10bn
- Building Society Deposits

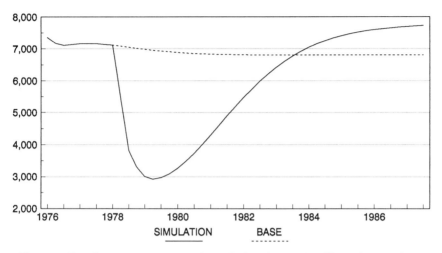

Figure 7F.5 Increase expected capital gain on dwellings by £10bn
- National Savings

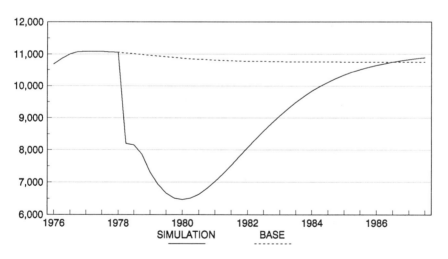

Figure 7F.6 Increase expected capital gain on dwellings by £10bn
- Public Sector Debt

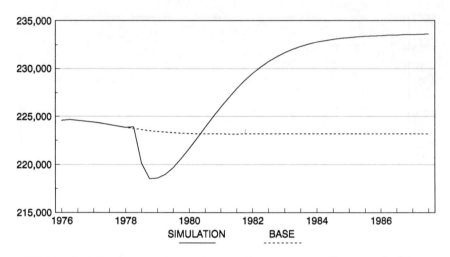

Figure 7F.7 Increase expected capital gain on dwellings by £10bn
- Dwellings

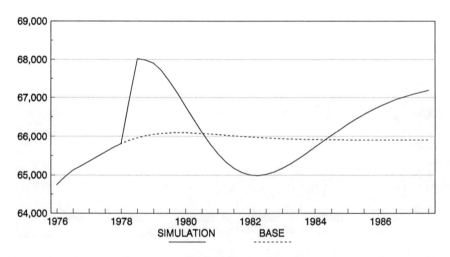

Figure 7F.8 Increase expected capital gain on dwellings by £10bn
- Consumer Durables

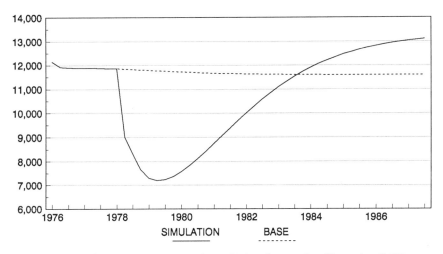

Figure 7F.9 Increase expected capital gain on dwellings by £10bn
- Consumer Credit

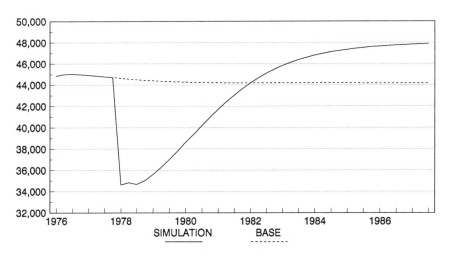

Figure 7F.10 Increase expected capital gain on dwellings by £10bn
- Loans for House Purchase

8 Conclusion

The objective of this study was to construct and estimate a model of household expenditure and asset accumulation for the period 1976 to 1987. The model which has been developed is an improvement on previous work on modelling household behaviour as it allows for a more varied set of interactions between real and financial decisions whilst overcoming many of the problems inherent in the systems approach to portfolio modelling.

After an examination of the theoretical background and previous empirical studies of household expenditure and portfolio decisions a decision was made to reject the commonly adopted assumption of separable preferences. Instead an integrated approach was used which allows for simultaneous inter-relationships between decisions during estimation. The estimated results of such a model were found to be encouraging and generally support the use of an integrated approach.

A number of problems relating to the modelling of personal sector behaviour were identified in the course of this study. These include the lack of a unified theory of consumption and portfolio behaviour and the problems of obtaining data which relates to households. For these and other reasons the majority of the empirical studies of personal sector behaviour have assumed separability of preferences. This has led to a body of empirical work on modelling consumption behaviour which is largely separate to the body of empirical work on modelling portfolio decisions and the portfolio models have been largely single equation models of only a part of the set of portfolio decisions. Recently though empirical work on modelling consumption behaviour has found a greater role for financial variables. In addition many recent models of portfolio decisions have attempted to develop systems of asset demand equations. There is therefore evidence of a movement in the direction of the integrated approach to modelling sectoral financial decisions. However there has still been very few attempts to integrate the modelling of consumption with asset demands. The few attempts that have been made have suffered from the traditional problems of systems modelling, namely large numbers of imprecise and wrongly signed parameters. Recent work on estimating systems of demand equations have shown that these problems can be mitigated by imposing the restrictions of homogeneity and symmetry derived form utility theory. Further to this it has been demonstrated that these restrictions are more often accepted when a general dynamic specification is adopted. The model developed in this research has benefited from these lessons. Further benefits have been derived from the use of the Granger - Engle two step approach to estimation. This allowed the construction of a plausible set of long run or desired demands before estimation of the dynamic model proceeded. The resulting integrated model is first of all an improvement on previous attempts to model personal sector behaviour in an integrated manner in that more precise and plausible estimates have been obtained. This has allowed the model to be used as a framework for simulation experiments. Secondly the model allows for and reveals, a more varied set of inter-relationships between expenditure and portfolio decisions than those permitted by separate models of the same behaviour. In particular the results of this study have suggested that separable modelling of capital certain and capital uncertain assets is not supported as the different parts of capital certain assets are not all substitutes or all complements as implied by the separable assumption. Also the results of the model provide support for the view that real assets can be modelled in the same way as financial assets with an own rate of return and further that real assets can be seen as substitutes to financial assets in the long run. A plausible consumption equation has also been obtained from this model which again supports the integrated approach and suggests in particular that adjustment of consumption to desired levels depends not only upon its own disequilibrium but upon a wider set of separate disequilibrium of assets and liabilities from desired stocks than is normally allowed for in consumption modelling.

The simulation experiments conducted using the model produced plausible results and therefore provide further support for the model. In addition the long run interest rate elasticities are broadly in line with similar studies of personal sector behaviour. The construction of the model with its varied set of interactions between real and financial decisions allows for the exploration of some interesting policy questions. One such question examined in this study was the effectiveness of different policies for controlling credit. It was found that the policy of direct controls on lending produced quicker and stronger effects on borrowing by the personal sector when compared to the alternative policy of raising interest rates. The results of the simulations also suggested that introducing terms controls on lending for house purchase (for example introducing a loan to value ratio) may be a more effective form of direct control than going back to quantity controls imposed on the balance sheets of lenders.

Therefore in overall conclusion the integrated approach to modelling personal sector behaviour, adopted in this study, has produced encouraging results. However there are criticisms which can be made of the study. The testing of the estimated model was not as thorough as it could have been, in particular there was no post sample tests. This however is inevitable in a heavily parametised model where degrees of freedom are scarce. There is also clearly further work required to improve the model as outlined at the end of chapter six. The usefulness of the model would be improved if some of the restrictions on relationships between real and financial decisions, excluded in the present model because of the potential for multicollinearity, could be removed. However the potential for further rewards from the use of the integrated approach has I believe been demonstrated.

Bibliography

Akerlof G A & Milbourne (1980) "The short run demand for money", Economic Journal, 90, 885-900

Anderson G J (1984) "The integration of portfolio and consumption decisions: even more pitfalls", Economics Department, Southampton University discussion paper no. 8322

Anderson G J & Blundell R (1982) "Estimation and hypothesis testing in dynamic singular equation systems", Econometrica, 70, 1559-71

Anderson G J & Blundell R (1983) "Testing restrictions in a flexible dynamic demand system: an application to consumers expenditure in Canada", Review of Economic studies, 50, 397-410

Anderson G J & Blundell R (1984) "Consumer non-durables in the UK: a dynamic demand system", Economic Journal (Conference papers), 35-44

Anderson G J & Hendry D F (1984) "An econometric model of United Kingdom Building Societies", Oxford Bulletin of Economics and Statistics, 46, 185-210

Backus D, Brainard W C, Smith G, Tobin J (1980) "A model of US financial and non-financial behaviour",

Journal of Money Credit and Banking, 12, 259-93

Backus D & Purvis D (1980) "An integrated model of household flow of funds allocations", Journal of Money Credit and Banking, 12, 400-21

Ball R J & Drake P S (1964) "The relationship between aggregate consumption and wealth", International Economic review, 5, 63-81

Bank of England Quarterly Bulletin (1982) "The supplementary special deposits scheme", 22

Barten A P (1969) "Maximum likelihood estimation of a complete system of demand equations", European economic review, 1, 7-73

Barclays Bank Review (1989, February)

Barr D G & Cuthbertson K (1988) "Modelling the flow of funds", Bank of England discussion paper, technical series No 21

Barr D G & Cuthbertson K (1989) "Econometric Modelling of the financial decisions of the UK Personal Sector: preliminary results", Bank of England discussion paper, technical series No 22

Barret K J, Gray M R, Parkin M (1975) "The demand for financial assets by the personal sector of the UK economy", in Modelling the Economy (ed. G A Renton), Heinemann

Baumol W J (1952) "The transactions demand for cash: an inventory theoretic approach", Quarterly Journal of Economics, 66, 545-556

Berndt E R, McCurdy T H & Rose D E (1980) "On testing theories of financial intermediary portfolio selection", Review of Economic Studies, 47, 861-73

Bewley R A (1979) "The direct equilibrium estimation of the direct response in a linear dynamic model", Economic Letters, 3, 357-61

Bewley R A (1981) "The portfolio behaviour of the London Clearing Banks:1963-71", Manchester School, 49, 191-200

Brainard W C & Tobin J (1968) "Pitfalls in financial model building", American Economic review, 58, 99-122

Buiter W H & Armstrong C A (1978) "A didactic note on the transactions demand for money and behaviour towards risk", Journal of Money Credit and Banking,

10, 529-38

Calder J R (1978) "The stock of consumer durables in the UK", Economic Trends, no. 239

Chang W W (1984) "On liquidity preference again: reply", American Economic Review, 74, 812-813

Christofides L N (1976) "Quadratic costs and multi-asset partial adjustment equations", Applied economics, 8, 301-5

Clower R W & Johnson M B (1968) "Income, wealth and the theory of consumption" in Wolfe N (ed), Value, Capital & Growth, Edinburgh University Press

Courakis A S (1975) "Testing theories of discount house portfolio selection", Review of Economic studies, 42, 643-8

Currie D & Kenally G (1985) "Personal Sector demand for liquid deposits in the UK", NIESR Discussion paper no. 100

Dalal A J (1983) "Comparitive statics and asset substitutability/complemenatary in a portfolio model: a dual approach", Review of Economic Studies, 50, 355-67

Davis E P (1984) "A recursive model of Personal Sector expenditure and Accumulation", Bank of England technical paper No 6

Davis E P (1987) "Rising sectoral debt income ratios: a cause for concern?", Bank for International Settlements, Economics Paper No. 20

Davis E P (1988) "Revaluations of Personal Sector assets", The Royal Bank of Scotland Review, September

de Leeuw F (1965) "A model of financial behaviour" in The Brookings Quarterly Econometric Model of the US economy (eds. J.S. Duesenberry, G Fromm, L Klein, and E Kuh), Rand McNally

Deaton A & Muellbauer J (1980a) "Economics and Consumer Behaviour", Cambridge University Press

Deaton A and Muellbauer J (1980b) "An almost ideal demand system", American Economic review, 70, 312-76

Diewert W E (1977) "Generalised slutsky conditions for aggregate consumer demand", Journal of economic theory, 15, 353-62

Davidson, Hendry, Srba, Yeo (1978) "Econometric modelling of the aggregate time series relationship between consumers expenditure and income in the United Kingdom", Economic Journal, 88, 661-92

Dicks M J (1988) "The interest elasticity of consumers' expenditure", Bank of England Discussion paper, technical series no. 20

Dreze J H & Modigliani F (1972) "Consumption decisions under uncertainty", Journal of Economic Theory, 5, 308-35

Engle R & Granger C W J (1987) "Cointegration and Error Correction: representation, estimation and testing", Econometrica, 55, 251-76

Engle R & Yoo B S (1987) "Forecasting and testing in co-integrated systems", Journal of Econometrics, 35, 143-159

Fuller W A (1976) "Introduction to time series analysis", Wiley

Friedman B (1977) "Financial flow variables and the short run determination of longterm interest rates", Journal of Political Economy, 85, 661-89

Friedman B & Roley V (1979) "Investors portfolio behaviour under alternative models of long term interest rate expectations: unitary, rational or autoregressive", Econometrica, 47, 1475-97

Goodhart C (1982) "Disequilibrium money - a note", Ch 10 in Monetary Theory and Practice, The UK experience, Macmillan

Gorman W M (1959) "Separable utility and aggregation", Econometrica, 27, 469-481

Granger C W J (1983) "Cointegrated variables and Error Correcting Models", UCSD Discussion Paper

Green C (1984) "Preliminary results from a five sector flow of funds model of the UK", Economic Modelling, 1, 304-26

Green and Keirnan (1989) "Multicollinearity and measurement error in econometric financial modelling", Manchester School, 57, 357-369

Grice J, Bennett A & Cumming N (1981) "The demand for sterling M3 and other aggregates in the UK", Treasury Working Paper No. 20 (August)

Hall R (1978) "Stochastic implications of the Life Cycle -

Permanent Income hypothesis: theory and evidence, Journal of Political Economy, 86, 971-987

Hall S (1986) "An application of the Granger Engle two step estimation procedure to United Kingdom aggregate wage data", Oxford Bulletin of economics and statistics, 48, 228-39

Hall S & Urwin R (1989) "A disequilibrium model of building society mortgage lending", Bank of England Discussion Paper, technical series no. 26

Harvey A C (1981) "The econometric analysis of time series", Philip Allan

Hendry D F (1983) "Econometric modelling: The Consumption Function in retrospect", Scottish Journal of Political Economy, 30, 193-220

Hendry D F & von Ungern-Sternberg T (1981) "Liquidity and inflation effects on consumers expenditure", in Essays in the theory and measurement of consumer behaviour in honour of Sir Richard Stone (ed Angus Deaton), Cambridge University Press

Hicks J R (1946) "Value and Capital: An Inquiry into some fundamental principles of economic theory", Oxford University Press

Hood W (1987) "The allocation of UK personal sector liquid assets", Government economic service working paper, 94

Jones T (1981) "The Household Sector", Economic Trends, September

Jump G (1980) "Interest rates, inflation expectations and spurious elements in measured real income and saving", American Economic Review, 70, 990-1004

Laidler D (1983) "The buffer stock notion in monetary economics", The Economic Journal - Supplement to Vol 94, 17-34

Markose S (1984) "Non-separability of consumption and portfolio choice with a precautionary demand for money", Greek Economic Review, 6, 171-202

McCallum B T (1976) "Rational Expectations and the natural rate hypothesis: some consistent estimates", Econometrica, 44, 43-52

Merton R C (1969) "Lifetime portfolio selection under uncertainty: the continuous time case", Review of

Economics and Statistics, 51, 247-57

Miller M H & Orr D (1966) "A model of the demand for money by firms", Quarterly Journal of Economics, 80

Miller M H & Orr D (1968) "The demand for money by firms: extensions of analytic results", The Journal of Finance, 23

Modigliani F & Brumberg R (1955) "Utility analysis and the consumption function : an interpretation of cross-section data" in Post Keynsian Economics, (ed. K K Kurihara), George Allen and Unwin

Owen P D (1981) "Dynamic models of portfolio behaviour: a general integrated model incorporating sequencing effects", American Economic review, 71, 231-8

Owen P D (1983a) "Wealth composition and cross equation effects in the UK personal sector's expenditure and portfolio behaviour", University of Reading discussion paper in economics, series A, no 142

Owen P D (1983b) "Invariance results for FIML estimation of an integrated model of expenditure and portfolio behaviour", University of Reading discussion paper in economics, series A no 143

Owen P D (1986) "Money, Wealth and Expenditure", Cambridge University Press

Parkin M (1970) "Discount House portfolio and debt selection", Review of economic studies, 27, 469-97

Parkin M, Gray M & Barrett R (1970) "The portfolio behaviour of commercial banks" in K Hilton & D Heathfield (eds), The Econometric Study of The United Kingdom, Macmillan

Patterson K D (1984) "Net liquid assets and illiquid assets in the consumption function", Economic Letters, 14, 389-395

Patterson K D (1985) "Income adjustments and the role of consumers' durables in some leading consumption functions", The Economic Journal, 95, 469-79

Patterson K D, Harnett I, Robinson G & Ryding J (1987) "The Bank of England Quarterly Model of the UK Economy", Economic Modelling

Pesaran H M & Evans R A (1984) "Inflation, Capital Gains and UK Personal Savings 1953-81", Economic Journal, 94, 237-257

Phillips A W (1954) "Stabilisation Policy in a closed economy", Economic Journal, 64, 290-32

Pissarides C A (1978) "Liquidity cosiderations in the theory of consumption", Quarterly Journal of Economics, 92, 279-96

Pratt M J (1980) "Building Societies: an econometric model", Bank of England Discussion Paper no. 11

Pudney S E (1981) "An empirical method of approximating the separable structure of consumer preferences", Review of Economic Studies, 48, 561-77

Purvis D (1978) "Dynamic models of portfolio behaviour:more on pitfalls in financial model building", American Economic review, 68, 403-9

Reid D J (1978) "The role of Personal Sector Balance Sheets in the National Accounting System and sources and methods used to compile them" in Personal Sector Balance Sheets and Current Developments in Inland Revenue Estimates of Personal Wealth, CSO Studies in Official Statistics no. 35

Roley V (1983) "Symmetry restrictions in a system of financial asset demands: theoretical and empirical results", Review of economics and statistics, 65, 124-30

Saito M (1977) "Household flow of funds equations: specificatiuon and estimation", Journal of Money, Credit and banking, 9, 1-20

Sargan J D (1964) "Wages and prices in the United Kingdom: A study in Econometric Methodology" in Hart et al (eds) Econometric Analysis for National Economic Planning, Butterworths

Sargan J D & Bhargava A (1983) "Testing residuals from Least Square regression for being generated by the Guassian random walk", Econometrica, 51, 153-74

Sheilds J (1988) "Controlling household credit", National Institute Economic Review, August, 46-55

Simmonns P (1980) "Evidence on the impact of income distribution on Consumer Demand in the UK, 1955-1968", Review of Economic Studies, 47, 893-906

Smith G (1975) "Pitfalls in financial model building: a clarificatiuon", American Economic Review, 65, 510-16

Smith G (1978) "Dynamic models of portfolio behaviour: comment on Purvis", American Economic review, 68,

410-16

Smith G & Brainard W (1976) "The value of a priori information in estimating a financial model", Journal of Finance, 31, 1299-322

Smith G & Brainard W (1982) "A disequilibrium model of savings and loan associations" Journal of Finance, 37, 1277-93

Spencer P D (1981) "A model of the demand for British Government stocks by non-bank residents 1967-77", Economic Journal,

Spiro A (1962) "Wealth and the consumption function",Journal of political economy, 70, 339-54

Sprenkle C M (1984) "On liquidity preference again - comment", American Economic Review, 74, 171-202

Stone R (1954) "The measurement of consumers expenditure and behaviour in the United Kingdom 1920-1938", Vol 1, Cambridge University Press

Stone R (1973) "Personal spending and saving in post war Britain" in Economic Structure and Development: Essays in honour of Jan Timbergen (ed H C Roe et al), North Holland

Stone J R N & Rowe D A (1957) "The market demand for durable goods", Econometrica, 25, 423-43

Strotz R H (1957) "The empirical implications of a utility tree", Econometrica, 25, 269-280

Strotz R H (1959) "The utility tree - a correction and further appraisal", Econometrica, 27, 483-488

Taylor C T & Threadgold A R (1979) " 'Real' national saving and its sectoral composition", Bank of England Discussion Paper No. 6

Taylor J & Clements K (1983) "A simple portfolio allocation model of financial wealth", European economic review, 23, 241-51

Tobin J (1956) "The interest elasticity of transactions demand for cash", Review of Economics and Statistics, 38, 241-247

Tobin J (1958) "Liquidity preference as behaviour towards risk", Review of Economic Studies, 25, 65-86

Tobin J (1972) "Wealth, liquidity and the propensity to consume" in Strumpel, Morgan & Zahn (eds), Human behaviour in economic affairs.

Tobin J & Dolde W (1974) "Wealth, liquidity and consumption" in Consumer spending and monetary policy: the linkages, Federal Reserve Bank of Boston

Toland S (1981) "Committed and Discretionary Saving", Economic Trends

Von Ungern-Sternberg T (1981) "Inflation and saving: international evidence on inflation induced income losses", Economic Journal, 91, 961-76

Weale M (1985) "Modelling the financial economy", Dept of applied economics, Cambidge, mimeo

Weale M (1986) "The structure of personal sector short term asset holdings", Manchester School, 54, 141-61

Webb R (1988) "Commodity Prices as Predictors of Aggregate Price Change", Economic Review, Federal Reserve Bank of Richmond

White W R (1975) "Some econometric models of deposit bank portfolio behaviour in the UK, 1963-70" in Modelling the Economy (ed. G A Renton) Heinemann

Wilcox J B (1985) "A model of the Building Society sector", Bank of England Discussion Paper no. 23

Yi G & Judge G (1988) "Statistical model selection criteria", Economic Letters, 28, 47-51